PHILIP JOHNSON
RECENT WORK

PHILIP JOHNSON, RITCHIE & FIORE ARCHITECTS

Architectural Monographs No 44

PHILIP JOHNSON RECENT WORK

Jeffrey Kipnis

This book is published
to honour the ninetieth anniversary of the birth of Philip Johnson
on 8 July 1906,
to celebrate his distinguished career
at the forefront of twentieth-century architecture

Front cover Gate House model and Berlin Alternative **Frontispiece** Berlin Alternative

Editor and Archivist for Philip Johnson, Ritchie & Fiore, New York Christian Bjone
Art Direction and Graphic Design 2 x 4, New York City

Attempts have been made to locate sources of all photographs and illustrations to obtain full reproduction rights, but in the very few instances where this process has failed to find the copyright holder, our apologies are offered. Unless otherwise stated all images are courtesy of the architect: **Illustration credits** Yasin Abdullah pp24-25, 62-63; Luis Blanc p26; Brett Bothwell pp77, 81; Frank O Gehry & Associates p108; Howard Associates pp112-13; Philip Johnson pp69, 109, 121; Gordon Kipping p74; John Manley pp22, 27, 44-45, 56-57, 72, 86-90, 99-101, 103-5, 108-9, 111; Elizabeth Murrell pp16, 18-19; Prestel Verlag, Munich, p117; Richard Schneider pp2, 42, 48-49; Duane Schrempp p76; Verlagsgemeinschaft Gerd/Hatje, Stuttgart, p60, above; **Photographic credits** Hedrich Blessing p125; Louis Checkman pp114; Isabel Colbrand/SAFI 2000 pp122-23; ESTO p68; David Harrison pp 27-31; Wolfgang Hoyt p75; Michael Moran pp32-39; Richard Payne p87, 90-92; Michael Rogul pp66-68; Robert Royal/Royal Productions p118; Rudolf Steiner Press, London, (photo: W Grunder), p61, left; Robert Walker pp17, 20-21, 23, 40-41, 46-47, 57, 95-98, 107-8; Joshua White/Frank O Gehry & Associates pp56, 59, 61-62, 102-3, 106

Architectural Monographs No 44

First published in Great Britain in 1996 by
ACADEMY EDITIONS
An imprint of

ACADEMY GROUP LTD
42 Leinster Gardens London W2 3AN
Member of the VCH Publishing Group

ISBN 1 85490 284 9

Distributed to the trade in the
United States of America by
NATIONAL BOOK NETWORK
4720 Boston Way Lanham Maryland 20706

Printed and bound in Singapore

I don't believe in principle, but, oh, I do believe in interest. J R Lowell

INTRODUCTION PART I

Recently, Philip Johnson presented his latest six projects to the students of Harvard's Graduate School of Design. During the discussion, a member of the audience asked a question that, in a certain sense, captured the entire problematic of Johnson's relationship to modernity in general and Modern/Post-Modern architecture in particular.

The student argued that every important figure in twentieth-century architecture – from Corb, Mies, Wright, and Kahn to Rossi, Venturi and Gehry – shared at least one characteristic. No matter how strongly they differed from one another, each of these architects maintained a single-minded philosophical/aesthetic integrity throughout his career, a level of commitment which the student termed the architect's 'central core'. Then, noting both the stylistic pluralism evident in the six projects as well as the architect's willingness to imitate the work of others, the student asked Johnson, 'beneath your eclectic tendencies, do you have a set of beliefs about architecture that you consider inviolate; in other words, do you have a central core?'

It was a poignant question, one sensitive to the fact that Johnson's aesthetic movements, exploitations and borrowings could not be simply dismissed as the any-style-for-sale packaging of commercial design. Johnson's renowned intellectual acuity and his lifetime of vigorous advocacy insist that, however one may assess them, his stylistic machinations deserved respect. At the very least, they deserved to be treated as having emerged from a well considered position on architecture.

Johnson replied, 'I don't know. Do I have a central core?' This quip is typical of the off-hand, ironic self-criticisms we have come to expect from the architect who is as famous for his declaration 'I am a whore' as for his legacy of incisive commentary. However, as is also typical of Johnson, this laconic response concentrates his position on one of the most profound and conflicted debates within architecture with precision and aphoristic force. In broadest terms, modernity is the scene which evolves out of the progressive frustration of the search for some incontestable arch-principle capable of grounding decisive arbitration. So accomplished are Western civilisation's accumulated techniques of sceptical demystification that each of the arch-principles that have for a time prevailed – God, Mankind, Self, Reason – have succumbed in their turn. Yet, throughout its history and in its very mythos, architecture conceives itself in essence as giving material form to such arch-principles. Thus, in a certain sense, the 'central core' of the major architects of the twentieth century can be understood as mounting a heroic resistance to the disestablishing momentum of modernity.

In these terms, to the question, 'do you have a central core?' modernity demands a 'no' while the architectural mythos commands a 'yes'. Thus, Johnson, who has always sought to be at once architect and Modernist, delivers the only answer possible for that most curious of oxymorons: the Modern architect. Throughout his career, Johnson has sought to resolve the contradiction by advocating the position that, as an art, architecture is entirely determined by the aesthetics of material form. According to Johnson, however much spirituality, ideology or theory may act as motives for the investigation of formal possibilities, in the end, none of these is ever actualised in material form. Design is only validated in the visual interest and experiential pleasure of the building. Thus the architect may avail himself of the entire catalogue of formal possibilities from historical quotation or imitation to the invention of new forms, in the service of aesthetic experience. No argument based on theoretical or ideological integrity can justifiably restrict the architect's palette.

In Western thought, aesthetic formalism was born in Kant's theory of disinterested beauty. Nietzsche, however, reshapes it into its virulent, modern form. Nietzsche rejects both Kant's view that beauty is a universal as well as his notion of disinterest ('Who looks at beauty in a disinterested way?'). This first philosopher of modernity then rewrites aesthetic formalism from the perspective of the artist: 'For the artist, form is content.' In a fundamentally modernist gesture, Nietzsche does not deny that form can convey ideological, theoretical, political or social meaning. He denies that such meanings are embodied in the object and therefore that they determine artistic responsibility at the expense of artistic freedom.

It is to Nietzsche's aesthetic that Philip Johnson has consistently appealed, however debatable his interpretation of these may be. Johnson is neither naive about architecture's political and social role nor disingenuous about design's capacity to engineer spiritual, ideological and theoretical effects. Rather, he is confirmed in his belief that aesthetics itself constitutes the artist's genuine theoretical and political activity. When accused of indulging in mere aesthetics, Johnson will always reply, 'what do you mean by "mere"?'

The most conspicuous evidence of Johnson's inclination to aestheticise is to be found in his treatments of Modernism in 'The International Style' (with Henry-Russell Hitchcock, 1932) and the new avant-garde in 'Deconstructivist Architecture' (in 1988 with Mark Wigley). In both cases, he went to some effort to present the design issues in strictly stylistic terms, largely ignoring the social and philosophical discourse that accompanied the development of each movement. This reduction of design to a question of style has enraged many, particularly Marxist historians and critics, who have indicted him for trivialising architecture by destituting it of its content in the service of bourgeois taste – no doubt to Johnson's endless delight. Johnson's pattern of aesthetic interpretation is reflected in the history of his own design activities, which amounts to an ongoing meditation upon prevailing stylistic themes. Indeed, his estate in New Canaan reads like a personal diary in which he has recorded his commentary on the architectural scene for over forty years. The six recent projects as well are no exception; each elaborates upon one or other motif that the architect derives from his interpretation of Deconstructivism.

The Slat House The architect's emphasis on the immediate experience is confirmed in the representation of his Slat House project. The work, a small garden structure, has no programme; consequently, Johnson approaches it as a sculptural opportunity. The Slat House is shown in site plan because of its significance as a visual turning element along the footpath. The elegant form belies its complex geometry in which a vertically lathed I- shaped wall intersects with a gestured, hyperbolic surface lathed horizontally over radiating supports. The result is a quiet, sophisticated structure that generates striking light/shadow and optical effects.

Lewis Guest House However much Johnson aspires to engage Deconstructivism, his tendency to resolve inherent tensions and contradictions into refined compositions is thoroughly Modern. The architect tempers this inclination somewhat in the Guest House, a basic study in the rotation, collision and intersection of regular volumes. Nonetheless, he avoids some of the more interesting difficulties, particularly as they arise in the interior. Always attentive to the pleasures of experience, Johnson is concerned more for such issues as sight lines, views and livable space than for confronting the more brutal possibilities of massed volumes as they protrude into one another. Thus, the architect resolves this problem by rotating the 'presence' of the cone and shaft in the cube's interior with skylights and benches. The brute force of the intersections is limited primarily to the elevations.

The difference between a more aggressive approach to the formal issues of Deconstructivism and Johnson's interpretation is summed up in his handling of the intersection of the north-east corner of the rotated cube and the existing structure. While the former demands that the difficult intersection be explored and elaborated upon, Johnson simply tidies up the problematic spaces with *poché*.

St Basil Chapel Responding to the client's desire for traditional symbolic form, Johnson mounts a hemispherical dome atop a cube to echo a Byzantine church. However, he shifts the dome off-centre, which results in two different effects. First, it allows the two ideal forms to retain some independence. Secondly, it positions the dome so that it may be sliced with greater effect, both in terms of the symbolic drama and in terms of the light reflected by the cut into the chapel. With the oblique slicing wall, Johnson makes an excellent use of a device borrowed from Tadao Ando and a lesson learned from Corb. Since Corb completed the chapels at Ronchamp and La Tourette, architects have begun to understand that one cannot grapple with the problem of producing sacred space in the context of modernity without making explicit use of profane gestures. Failing to confront that issue almost invariably leads to unacceptably sentimental results. Johnson solves several spatial problems at once with the wall. First, in one and the same gesture he offends the symbolic form of the chapel and produces a virtual narthex. This act of destruction/construction cleaves the space and activates the passage from the profane to the sacred. The problematic residual spaces resulting from the intersection are essential to the effect and, in this case, the architect is careful to allow them to remain unmoderated. The slicing wall also serves to resuscitate an otherwise banal courtyard threatened by the constraints of the site. It links the chapel to the galleries with *ad hoc* suture rather than ideal and resolved connection. Then, in combination with the peeled entry, the perforated slicing wall layers the space and undermines the cliché of a strong facade at the terminus. The result is a dispersed, eddying space whereas one would normally expect the space to be focused and abruptly terminated. It suggests that the chapel is not so much a grand finale to the processional as an important but provisional episode along the path.

Seton Hill Fine Arts Center
'Immature poets imitate; mature poets steal', wrote TS Eliot and in this design for a Fine Arts school we find Johnson in his wittiest maturity. As all will recognise, Johnson's scheme is a paraphrase of Frank Gehry's Winton House, which, of course, is an addition to a house Johnson designed. When confronted with the two projects during his Harvard lecture, Johnson quietly studied the two schemes for a moment. Then turning to the audience, he announced, 'Clearly, I did it better.'

The impetus for Johnson's assessment flows primarily from the difference in the spatial qualities of the two projects. Both schemes ruminate upon certain aspects of medieval Tuscan villages such as San Gimignano. Gehry abstracts the forms and then shrinks the village to the unlikely scale of the house. Thus, his scheme achieves its interest by intensifying the clutter and formal incongruity inherent in the village.

Johnson, on the other hand, takes advantage of the institutional programme to situate the scale of his miniature between the extremes of the original and Gehry's toy version and to recall something of the form/function relationships of the village. Furthermore, by reiterating some of the characteristic gestures and inflections, Johnson restores the historical flavour Gehry is so careful to erase. Hence, although Johnson loses the spirited clash and inconsonance that is at the heart of Gehry's scheme, he recaptures precisely those spatial qualities of the village the architect prefers, such as the meandering processional and the loosely organised accretion of *ad hoc* forms. The result is a gentle, picturesque project that could not be more appropriate to the context and programme.

Law Center Addition, University of Houston To the orthodox Deconstructivist, however, praise that includes the words 'could not be more appropriate to the context and programme' would ring a discordant alarm. After all, Deconstructivism begins as an ambivalence about received notions of architectural propriety. Insofar as Deconstructivism aspires to any relationship to Derrida's Deconstruction, the notion of ambivalence becomes increasingly important. In its strictest terms, Deconstruction does not call for the confrontational attack on systems of propriety mounted by the traditional avant-garde. Rather, it calls for occupying those systems in a way which both subverts and maintains their mechanisms. This goal is accomplished by exploiting the vulnerable nodes of internal ambivalence every system harbours.

In many ways, Johnson's memorable scheme for the Law Center approaches that goal. As we read the project in different interpretive frames, we find the characteristic trait of Deconstruction: a received system of propriety at once confirmed and denied. Some care must be exercised here, for such a reading requires that the tradition of restricting critical argument to evaluating the intentions of the architect and to examining whether or not those intentions are successfully embodied in the design must be suspended. No claim is made that the following readings constitute evidence for a keener, cannier Johnson. Rather, what might be claimed is that a stroke of luck, a chance combination of circumstance, programme and aesthetic disposition produces uncanny results.

As in the Glass House and Seton Hill, Johnson atomises the Law School programme into separate pavilions, enabling him to transform what would have been *building plan and section* entirely into *site section/elevation*. The site plan is straight Constructivism, while the elevation is dominated by Deconstructivist idioms, such as the great, tilted canopy reminiscent of Libeskind's Berlin 'Skyprop' or Eisenman's gridded loggia at the Wexner Center.

The canopy bullies its way through the individual buildings, cutting through them and knocking them off normal in both the horizontal and vertical planes while at the same time crudely stapling them together. In this case, Johnson is less than polite, as his aggressive treatment of the site section and detailing of the canopy's various intersections confirm.

The relationship between the plan and elevation is but the first of the subverted/maintained relationships that permeate this project. Though the plan and elevation are in every way coherent, nevertheless, the orthogonal extrusion implied by the Constructivist plan is subverted in the elevational obliques, and the dominant-axis character of the elevation is belied in the multi-vectored geometry of the plan.

In a spatial sense, there is no Law Center building as such that one can simply enter and leave. Rather, the project essentially consists of rooms (the buildings) branching off a partially enclosed hallway (the canopied walkway). Thus, one is never quite inside or outside the Law Center, an effect that extends even to the tenting which provisionally roofs the plaza. Subverting while maintaining traditional inside/outside relationships is, of course, perhaps the most important of Deconstruction tactics. When one considers that the very basis of jurisprudence is the ability to decide meaning with unambiguous clarity – to negotiate inside/outside relationships decisively – the Deconstruction Johnson's project effects on the space of the institution of a Law Center becomes all the more acute.

One might even elaborate the studied ambivalence of the project in a narrative reading. The great tilted canopy ostensibly points to the future location of the George Bush Presidential Library. One interpretation of the canopy is to denote a gesture of respect from the social foundations of law to the loftier task of politics. On the other hand, the tilted canopy can be read as the burden of George Bush's politics crashing down on the noble domain of the law. Thus, both Democrats and Republicans alike have their symbolic aspirations for the project at once confirmed or denied.

Whether or not one attributes these readings to Johnson's intentions is of little consequence. What is clear is that Johnson's experiments with the formal language of Deconstructivism, tempered by his inclination to good manners, in this case collaborated with the good fortunes of programme and context to engender marvellous effects in subversion and maintenance. In these terms, the Law Center stands with the very best of the architect's work.

As we survey these projects and admire their energy and range we nonetheless cannot ignore how often Johnson employs his facility to ease the more acute tensions and tame the more aggressive possibilities of the formal motifs he examines. For better or worse, the architect returns again and again to the aesthetic criteria he developed during his Modernist period: the resolved composition, the pre-eminence of the processional, the importance of perception and so on. This recurring appeal to prior standards inevitably mollifies the quirks and deviations he puts into play and smacks more of a Kantian than a Nietzschean attitude. Moreover, one should notice that the intellectual discourse that Johnson ignores while he plunders the formal spoils of Deconstructivism enabled other architects to ward off these domesticating tendencies.

On the other hand, even if Philip Johnson may be one of the very few architects with the acumen to feel a sting at being accused of falling back on such traditional themes as beauty and good taste, one imagines he has known what he was doing all along and, moreover, was damned pleased with himself and the results. One might even say that such contentment constitutes his 'central core'.

When last I wrote about Philip Johnson's work, he was busy indulging his new interest in a Deconstructivist aesthetic. Already, the doyens of architectural propriety had railed against his MOMA Deconstructivist exhibition. As they would have it, the incorrigible Johnson had chopped and stuffed the irreducible diversity of such solitary figures as Libeskind, Eisenman and Koolhaas into a paper-thin pseudo-category, like a butcher stuffs farce into cowgut to make sausage. Just to satisfy his insatiable appetite for publicity.

INTRODUCTION PART II

As if to provoke his critics even further, Johnson began his own Decon experiments, reducing the esoteric procedures of the original architects to a few simple-to-apply formal tactics – fragments, non-orthogonal angles, aggressive, dissonant intersections – that any architect could employ without bothering to master one or another arcane theory. Of course, university students and not a few professionals had found the same formula earlier. But Johnson, according to those same doyens, would go too far. He would refine Decon to make it more palatable and package it as a novelty for sale to corporate and institutional clients. God forbid.

At any rate, those early efforts occasioned the previous essay. In it, I used the opportunity of Johnson's notorious stylistic caprice to revisit a conflict between a founding fable of the architect and the dynamic of modernity. The conflict in question pits the fable of the architect as a man with a singular, ennobling vision pursued with unshakable conviction, against the understanding that modernity, in its broadest sense, is that complex of economic, political and intellectual mechanisms whose primary characteristic is to undermine continuously the grounds upon which such convictions rest. Johnson emerged from that essay posed against the fabled architect as a quintessential Modern, for better or worse.

Now, after only a few years, I return to find a new batch of Johnsons. While one or two of these bring to a conclusion his Deconstructivist play, the preponderance announces yet another change in style. On first view, these latter projects such as the Berlin Alternative and the Gate House seem merely to indicate a new affection on the part of the architect for Expressionist form and materiality. Yet, the more closely we examine the emergence and evolution of these projects, the more we discover that this shift marks a fundamental change in Johnson's approach to architecture, a change unlike any other in the architect's forty-plus-years career.

However intriguing this new work is, we must not neglect Johnson's achievement in his last Deconstructivist project (as consultant to John Burgee architects). The Puerto de Europa consists of a pair of leaning towers straddling the Paseo de la Castellana to form a gateway to the Plaza de Castilla in Madrid. The design of the Puerto de Europa is emblematic of a familiar mode of Johnsonian debauchery wherein the architect corrupts an innovative design device to produce an effect that undermines the cultural ambition for which the device was originally developed. The most famous example is Johnson's adulteration of Mies' Modernist vocabulary of form and transparency into the traditional domestic space of the Glass House. Similarly, in the Puerto de Europa, Johnson uses one of Decon's most aggressive tactics, tilting off the orthogonal, to reinforce a dominant urban axis and to establish a primary symbolic entry onto the plaza. The hierarchical effect is, of course, thoroughly antagonistic to the original disestablishing agenda of Deconstructivist architecture.

The cinematographic drama of the Puerto derives from a montage of two incongruent effects: the abstract, gravity-defying spectacle of a leaning tower and the compelling symbolic image that the mirrored symmetry engenders, suggesting, for example, a sabre salute to the passage of royalty. The result is a more effective contemporary solution to a traditional urban problem than Von Spreckelsen achieved with his techno-cover of an old formal standard at the Grand Arch in Paris.

The Puerto de Europa is one of Johnson's strongest designs in years, so it is somewhat surprising to find him abandoning its line of inquiry for an entirely different, more organic formal language. It is almost as if Johnson's interest in a new style ebbs precisely when he finds himself able to rein its most fugitive effects into the service of quotidian architectural convention. Ever fascinated by the new, Johnson nevertheless appears compelled perpetually to make the new serve the commonplace. Yet, even if we could elaborate this speculation into a convincing account of the waxing and waning of Johnson's interests, we would not have broached the broader implications of such individual inconstancy.

In the face of the forces of modernity, every commitment to principle must give way to the vicissitude of interests, structured always and inevitably as fascination terminating in boredom. When individual interests spontaneously coalesce, the emergent organisation is called a fashion, the most powerful and widely disparaged of all collective effects.

However much we lament the fact, in modernity fashion supplants permanent allegiance (to truth, to beauty, to ideology, etc) as the pre-eminent source of motive for all cultural production, whether art or science. Moreover, the conclusion of the argument at its limit is inexorable: in the wake of modernity, fashion stands as the only remaining authentic political form. The consequences of this state of affairs is obvious to all who follow today's media politics. Whether it is cause to celebrate fashion or to revile politics is one of the defining questions of our era.

In any case, whatever other damnations may have been heaped upon Johnson, no one has ever denied the architect's mastery of fashion and its ability to mesmerise the media; and not since the AT&T Building, or possibly even the Glass House itself, has this mastery been so in evidence as with the architect's Gate House in New Canaan. Within months of its completion, the Gate House, a tour de force of his new style, received an astonishing level of media attention, particularly for so small a building.

A genius for fashion is not a gift for originality; rather, it is an ability to intuit and act upon a welling of interest that may have been in formation for some time. Throughout his career, Johnson has not only been conspicuously unoriginal, he has, by virtue of his habitual rostering of references, positioned himself against the myth of architectural originality. So, it is no surprise for Johnson to find his way to his new-found interest through the work of others. What is telling, however, is the path he took – and the turns he avoided.

The first hint of drift appeared in the second of the three proposals for the Lewis Guest House, a cameo project within Frank Gehry's overall design. Ostensibly responding to the client's inclination towards the erotic, Johnson abandoned the crashing cubes motif of the first design in favour of a pear form inscribed within a box. After three years of single-minded dedication to one stylistic premise, however, the sudden appearance of so different an attitude could not simply be attributed to client-driven expediency. Johnson was tiring of Decon. Even if the pear scheme was little more than a Pop Art sketch, a clever, if cloying, temporisation, its sinuous form augured the direction to come.

Johnson found his bearings a short time later during a visit to Frank Stella's studio, where some wax maquettes of the artist's design for the Dresden Museum caught his eye. At Stella's urging, Johnson took the models back to his studio and began exploring them in a series of study projects. When finally ready to proclaim his latest fascination to the world, he chose one of these studies for an unveiling staged, as is his custom, with unrivalled panache.

'1930's Berlin is where I awoke', says Johnson, 'not just to architecture, but to life.' Thus, when invited to design an office building on the Friedrichstrasse in 1990, he thought it would be the project of a lifetime. In 1993, near the building's completion, Johnson went to Berlin to deliver the prestigious Bertelsman Lecture. Among the glitterati in attendance was Dr Hans Stimmann, the city's controversial Baudirektor.

Stimmann maintains a steadfast view of the past and future urbanism of Berlin. He has stated, for example, that the two worst influences on Berlin were Mies van der Rohe and Hans Scharoun. Working with a small but zealous cadre of architects, historians and intellectuals, Stimmann has spearheaded a set of urban design regulations intended to restore physical Berlin to its pre-Modern state, or a caricature thereof. During Johnson's work on the building, he ran headfirst into these regulations, which he obeyed dutifully, if somewhat glassy-eyed. As a result, the building, whatever its merits, did not approach the architect's original aspirations.

With his Bertelsman Lecture, Johnson secured a modicum of redress. At the end of a moving talk that drew upon personal reminiscences to effect a critical commentary on the urbanism of Berlin, Johnson turned his attention towards Stimmann. With the politesse of an elder statesman and the chutzpah of a PR huckster, Johnson offered the Baudirektor a comparison of the building he built with the building he would liked to have built: the Berlin Alternative. The audience, and the press, erupted, animated in equal measure by the striking, undulant form of the project and by the genteel but unmistakable upbraiding of Stimmann.

The Berlin Alternative is a stunning variation on a theme by Stella. In it, we can already see the uncanny gestural qualities that link this body of current work – by Johnson and others – to a history of Expressionist architecture, while at the same time distinguishing it from that history as something quite different. But for all of the bravura of the performance, it relied more on trickery than architecture for its success.

Johnson bewitched the audience with beautiful, computer-rendered perspectives of the form, showing minute people to give the immense scale of the project and suggesting a dream-like reality. These hypnotic images frame it as a sublime, freestanding sculpture afloat on an endless ocean of space. Each is crafted to emphasise the most desirable qualities of the gestural form. No fenestration, no materiality, no other buildings in context are allowed to compromise the images. To secure a false credibility for the project, Johnson moved quickly to show technical line drawings of the form as a rigorously measured building on site.

Though intoxicated by the form, the architect was still far from controlling its architecture. In fact, in some of his early studies, Johnson attempted to work out the fenestration, materiality and construction of these forms with such little success that he temporarily abandoned the Stella studies to pursue another, more familiar tactic. For his final effort on the Lewis Guest House, he would disinter and attempt to reanimate a project from architectural history.

The procedure had already worked well for Johnson. After all, there is no more reliable a technique to acquire new skills than to copy, a secret known well to the likes of Alberti, Bach, Shakespeare and Scorsese. By turning to the past, he could benefit from the experience and expertise of other architects exploring similar problems.

Unfortunately, the architect alit upon the most vapid of the German Expressionists, Hermann Finsterlin. During the forty years that Johnson openly deplored Expressionist architecture, he had typically singled out Finsterlin for scorn. Thus, though baffling, Johnson's choice was no accident. That it was a blunder, on the other hand, seems clear. By reproducing the inelegant original with meticulous verisimilitude, the architect begot a bleached blob that resembled nothing so much as a giant, albino octopus.

But why rob the grave of history at all? If unsure of the architectonics of the Stella studies, why not turn to kindred contemporaries, to Frank Gehry or Peter Eisenman for example? Johnson already had quoted each before: Gehry at Seton Hill, Eisenman at the CBC Building in Toronto. Moreover, he credited Eisenman's Max Reinhardthaus and Gehry's Disney Concert Hall for arousing his current interest.

Vanity surely had a role in this curious detour, particularly since the Guest House would be situated within a Gehry design. In addition, Johnson, ever cautious, relished the safety net of historical validation, a useful prop for one so wary of venturing out on a limb. But most importantly, to this day, he remains a rationalist who searches for reductive principles and simple techniques to guide his design, even when that design must look irrational. To Johnson's mind, the abstruse processes employed by those presently working in this area are repugnant obfuscations and mystifications.

Johnson's mind: too restless for scholarship, too patrician for science. Too erudite, too clear, too acute to tolerate the ineradicable occult that quickens art, that is art. In truth, Johnson does not possess the mind of an artist. His career is brilliant testimony to a fixation on the art of architecture and to the power of a perverse will to imitate its effects. For four decades he has conquered new architectures by turning them into formulae, a formidable legacy, but one that belongs less to an artist than to an intellectual.

But by endeavouring to use German Expressionism as a pattern-book, Johnson made a miscalculation more fundamental than the merely imprudent choice of Finsterlin. He assumed that the forms he sought were all members of a single category, Expressionism, and counted on the past to teach him its design formula. In so doing, he fell into one of architectural history's most insidious traps, for, of all of its categories, Expressionism is the most specious.

Of course, historical periods and styles are always open to question. No categorical nominative, however carefully defined, has sufficient tensile strength to bind disparate practices into a simple ensemble of similarity, unambiguously distinct from others. Nevertheless, such collective terms are useful, particularly when they elaborate broad affinities in technique, form, and effect, such as to be found in Wölfflin's treatment of the Baroque.

But no such detailed elaboration exists for the notion of architectural expressionism, which merely compiles forms of gesture and inflection, without regard to technique or effect. In this sense, the notion performs the same trivial task of categorical linkage for architectural form that a garbage truck does for its contents; and for much the same reason.

The category is indifferent to the wide variety of design techniques explored by so-called Expressionists; indeed, it is wholly uninterested in the question of actual technique at all. Instead, it perpetuates a legend of personal, expressive intent through ineffable gesture, a legend uncorroborated by a single significant architectural example. Because it ruthlessly disregards effects, it expunges crucial distinctions. We no longer discriminate among Scharoun's architecture of existential politics, the Taut brothers' Post-Futurism and Finsterlin's fanciful naturalism. They are all just German Expressionists, concocters of frivolous form.

Even as a stylistic category, architectural expressionism is so broadly drawn that it engulfs much of an entire century of atypical projects effortlessly. It identifies only non-rectitude; its 'tin eye' sees no relevant difference between curvilinear, faceted or inflected forms. Thus, it is unable to offer germane insights into works by Gaudí, Aalto, late Corb, Gehry, Domenig, Shirdel, Libeskind, Eisenman or Hadid, to name a few of those credited with expressionist projects.

If architecture is a visual art, then a certain style of question about the visual interest of form should be decisive for his current investigation. Why does Scharoun's faceted Philharmonic remain *au courant*, while Bruno Taut's faceted designs flounder *démodés*? Why did the stealth fighter look so cool, while the stealth bomber looked so ordinary? Why do Gehry's wiggles and blobs look chic, while Domenig's look 'geek'? Why are Stella's forms hot, and Finsterlin's not? Even if the more probative issues of technique and effect are set aside, theoretical treatments of expressionism as style should at least broach these questions, but do not.

A category so inept is no category at all. It is a place-holder, an empty cipher used to store and render inoffensive the garbage that many critics and historians wish would disappear but cannot eradicate.

Why? An impossible question to answer conclusively, but a few possibilities suggest themselves. First, the wanton excess of such architectures undermines the semantic, syntactic and typological rigour that structures mainstream architecture. Secondly, these architectures operate at the frontiers of the field, weakening its border to unwanted encroachment by the sculptural, the camp and the kitsch. Finally, they confront the discipline with its own essential visuality. In so doing, they expose the conservative agendas that underwrite traditional architectural aesthetics and, at the same time, disenchant a liberal desire for a dematerialised architecture that transcends form. In short, they sabotage the foundations of the prevailing modes of architectural judgement.

Johnson's outspoken opinions on the work of other architects can change in the blink of an eye. Not one to flatter himself, he must surely be as mercurial in his personal assessment of his own works. In public, however, even among friends, Johnson maintains an informal, but dignified loyalty to each one of his buildings and projects. Accordingly, he remains a staunch enthusiast for the Lewis Guest House. 'I love it. I think it is splendid', he flatly asserts. On the other hand, at the very next opportunity, he returned to the Stella studies with a vengeance.

Johnson came away from the Guest House better equipped to tackle the architectural problems that stumped him in the Berlin Alternative. Concrete injection eased his uncertainty about construction. The method forced the architect to abandon his original aspiration to build the complex forms in curtain wall, an idea that promised intriguing plays of changing materiality and transparency. In compensation, the technique gave Johnson almost unlimited freedom of form.

Injection also enabled the architect to pay special attention to the arrisses, the ridges and hips formed by surfaces intersecting in an exterior angle. The arris is a classical architectural problem, evolving from the design of a Doric column's fluting. To rediscover it as an intrinsic aspect of his new style must have been a particular pleasure for the architect, who so enjoys reminding every avant-garde of its debt to history.

Now confident that his abilities matched his ardour, Johnson decided to build one of the Stella studies at the renowned Glass House in New Canaan, scene of the architect's intimate reflections on the last half-century of architecture. Whether his own status in architectural history is best understood as an artist or an intellectual may be debated, but that of the Glass House compound is beyond doubt. As a whole, it is an incomparable masterwork, an attribution that obtains as well to several of its individual buildings, including the Sculpture Gallery and the Glass House itself. It is, therefore, an imposing context for any new construction. As the Gate House is only recently finished, assessment of its status relative to the other pavilions would seem hasty. Yet, in my opinion, it is already clear that it will stand among the very best.

I can offer no more accurate a description of its visual impact than this: the Gate House astonishes. It shocks the eye on every subsequent encounter as much as it does on the first. What the Glass House achieves in exquisite and serene sobriety, the Gate House attains in intrigue and voluptuous seduction. The former is rational quiescence; lulling one into tranquil reverie. The latter is erotic perturbation itself, driving one into an endless dance of circumnavigation, like Mephisto's violin. They are the Apollonian and the Dionysian. Johnson's life-long obsession with Nietzsche becomes manifest, and at long last, the Glass House is complete.

Keenly aware that the violent contrast between the Glass House and the Gate House threatened the fragile balance of the compound, Johnson sited the Gate House so that the visitor cannot see the Glass House from it, and so that it is the only pavilion on the property that cannot be seen from the Glass House. But Johnson, who lives in the Glass House on weekends, has a voracious appetite for his newest creation. He is, at this moment, wrestling recklessly with an addict's compulsion to remove the trees that screen the two from each other.

Typical of Johnson's built work, the Gate House is utterly refined; every nuance, from the graceful swelling and thinning of arrisses to the fastidious satin plaster finish, is wrought with sophistication. Unlike the Glass House, however, it is not a work of consummate perfection. The Caligarian window and door are notably awkward, for example, and the architect was wise to keep them to a minimum, one of each.

The design task of penetrating such forms is exacting and may not be solvable in general, though there are some exceptional cases of success, for example at Ronchamp. Windows and doors tend to operate as elements and contribute to the usually desirable effect of making a building appear as a composition of multiple elemental systems. Alternatively, with complex forms the desired effect is organic coherence. Windows and doors that look added and/or composed compromise the result. Ideally, either transparency should be integral to the construction of the form, or openings that serve as windows and doors should be inherent to the form, eg, as labiation or fissuring. The difficulty has been well known for some time; perhaps it is why Mies van der Rohe avoids the issue in his two Berlin High Rise studies of 1920-21.

Organic coherence need not mean monotonic nor monolithic. Indeed, these two characteristics contribute to the failings of the Lewis Guest House. The brachiate form reveals its entire logic to any and every view, an effect amplified by its white surface and its radial organisation. The Gate House is cannier. The building consists of two lobes, red and black, congenitally united like Siamese twins. As one moves around it, the flexed and undulating forms constantly conceal and reveal partial views of one another. With every stride, the view of the forms and colours shifts fluidly into a new configuration.

On the interior, a neutral steel grey unifies the two lobes and wrests the volume from a simple congruence with the exterior form, a disquieting result augmented by the dynamics of the changing wall thickness. Here, too, the achievement is far more sophisticated than at the Lewis Guest House. In the latter project, as soon as one sees the building, one knows the interior volume immediately. The skylight *oculi* on top of each arm confirm what the form blandly announces: the interior volume is but a thinly disguised modelling of an extruded room plan.

Perhaps the most wondrous quality of the Gate House is its continuous unfolding of undesigned effects. The shadows cast by the warped forms on the ground and on one another shift and twist anew from hour to hour, as if they had minds and bodies of their own. Rem Koolhaas visited during a early morning rain shower. He now recounts being mesmerised by the mist and water as they writhed off the building. As I said, the Gate House astonishes.

I have already speculated that Johnson grows bored with and abandons styles as soon as he is sufficiently in control of them to make them serve prosaic ends. Does his splendid achievement at the Gate House, then, imply that the architect's excursion into complex form has peaked? A quick look at the strange Korean Museum project, with its radiating, extruded ovals and grand central axis, suggests otherwise. The scheme is by no means uninteresting, but if it is intended in any way to reflect his new style, it is obvious that he has not even begun to work out the problems of designing large institutional buildings using complex form.

On the other hand, if there exists a single thing in the world that Johnson loves more than designing, it would be getting commissions. Like any architect worth his mettle, his avarice in this area knows no bounds. Thus, Johnson rarely does competitions; they are just too risky. When he does, he goes all out for the win. Perhaps the Korean Museum scheme was the best compromise he could reach between his current interests and his desire to win a very conservative contest.

When considering the Turning Point memorial in Cleveland, the answer is less clear. The gestured stelae produce one particularly fascinating effect: as the external viewing angle changes, the twisting forms fluctuate between appearing atavistic and contemporary. Yet, inside, certain worrisome routines of good taste are creeping back, such as its representational inference of Stonehenge, or its typology of a sacred precinct delimited by a tetrastyle. Only the baldachin is missing.

Peaking or peaked? We will have just have to wait for the next bunch of Johnsons to find out.

TURNING

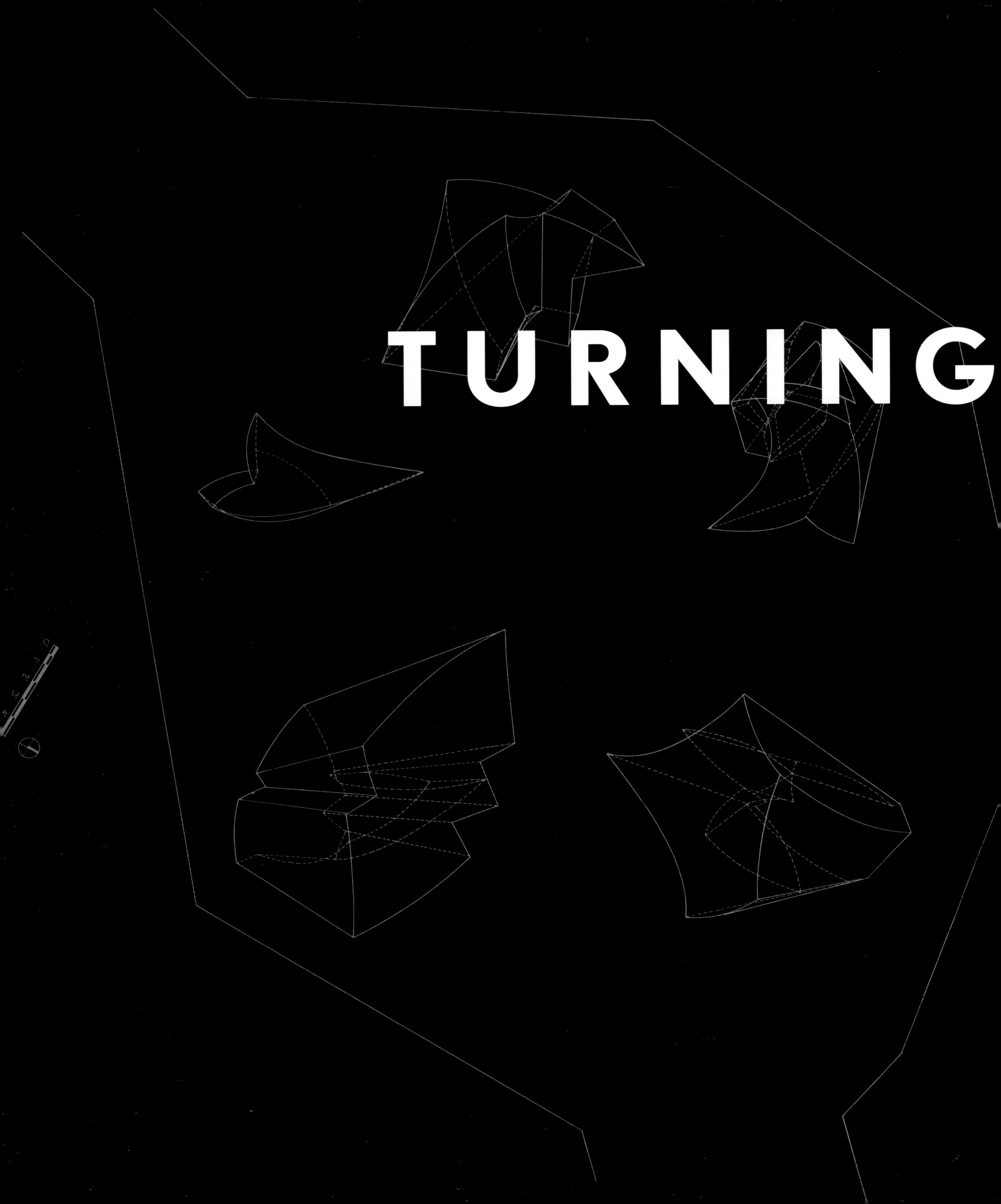

Aerial view of plaster study model

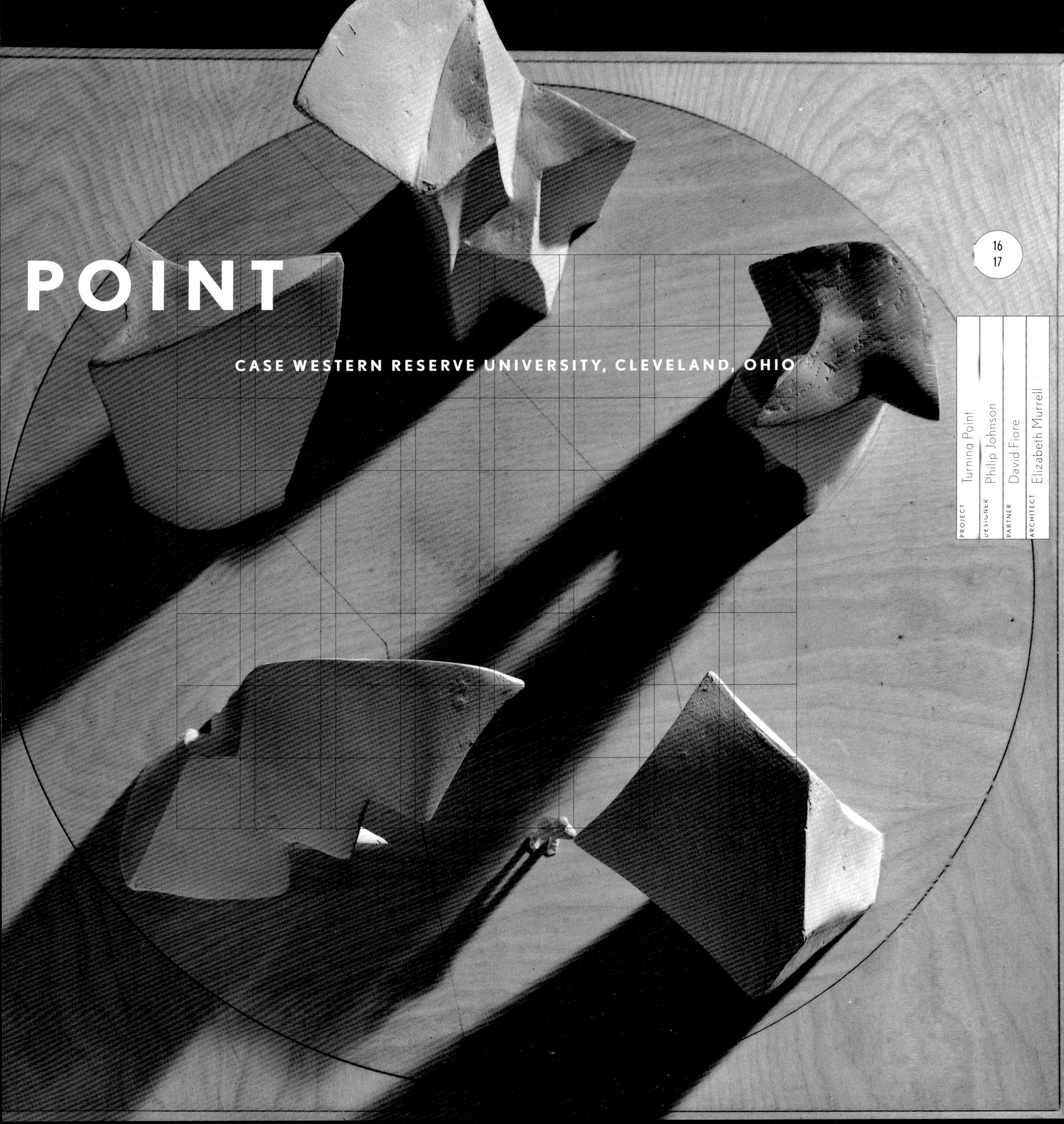

POINT

CASE WESTERN RESERVE UNIVERSITY, CLEVELAND, OHIO

PROJECT Turning Point
DESIGNER Philip Johnson
PARTNER David Fiore
ARCHITECT Elizabeth Murrell

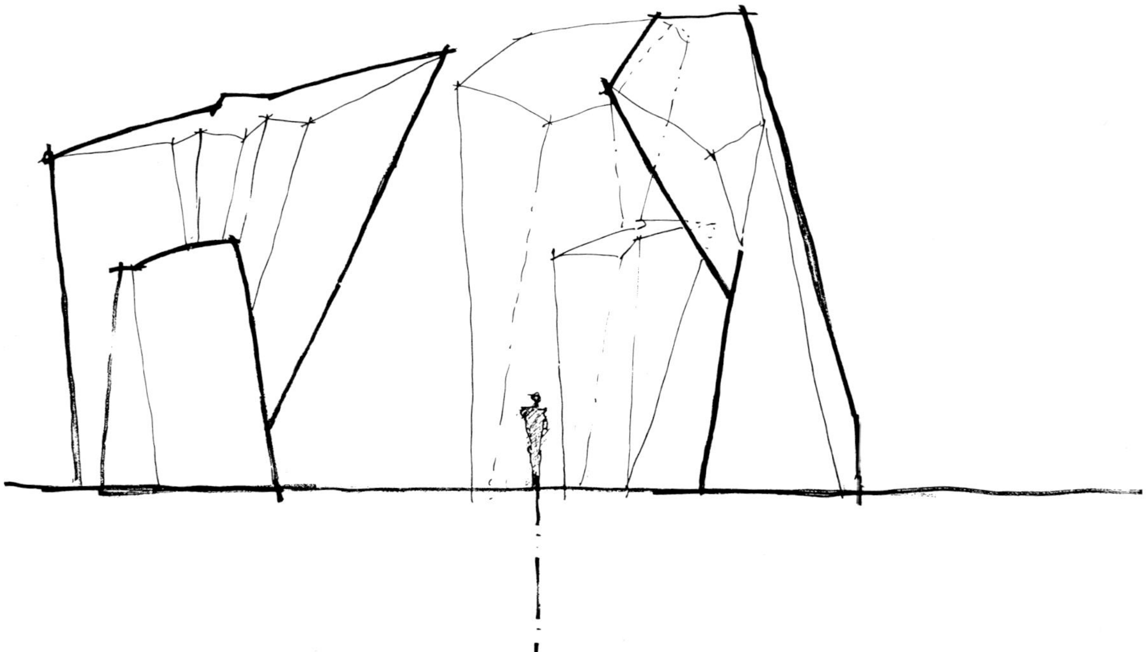

1996

T U R N I N G P O I N T is an architecture composed of five sculptural forms organised around the turning point of a campus pedestrian path. The shapes, each approximately six metres in height and varying from one to five metres in width, converge and diverge around an illusive focal point. The individual shapes will be constructed in polyester resin and fibreglass formed over structurally reinforced polyurethane foam, a process utilising the latest computer technology and traditional craftsmanship. The final forms will be sheathed in a pigmented elastomeric coating, in the pale hues of earth, stone and bone. While individually sculptural, the objects are meant to be experienced as elements of architecture and reflect a long-standing preoccupation with procession and monumentality. Pedestrians travelling through the monument encounter the thwarted suggestions of arches, volumes and voids before passing to the other side. Night lighting for the project is similarly other-worldly, utilising fibre optics radiating from a central origin, like moonlight, which illuminate the interior faces of the structure.

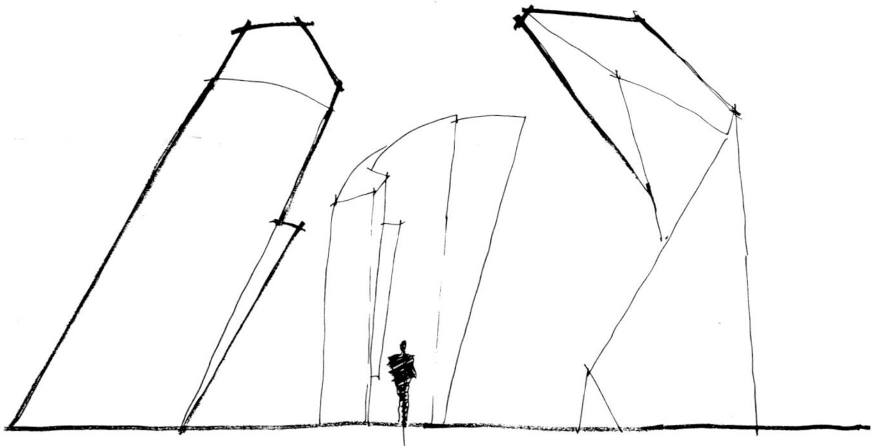

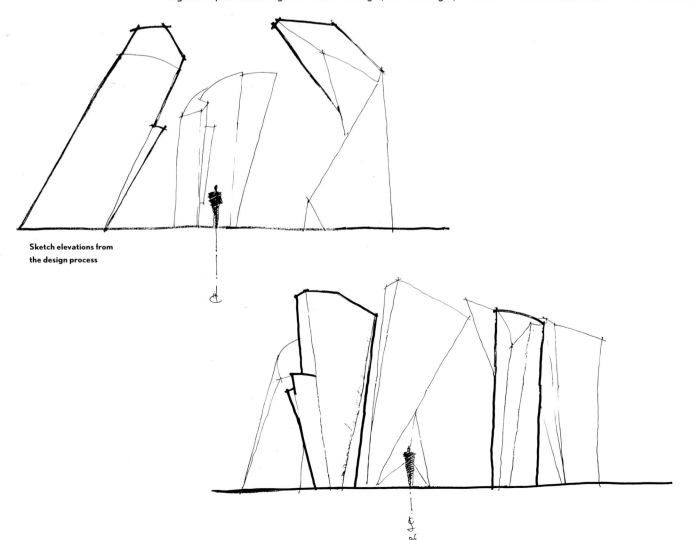

Sketch elevations from the design process

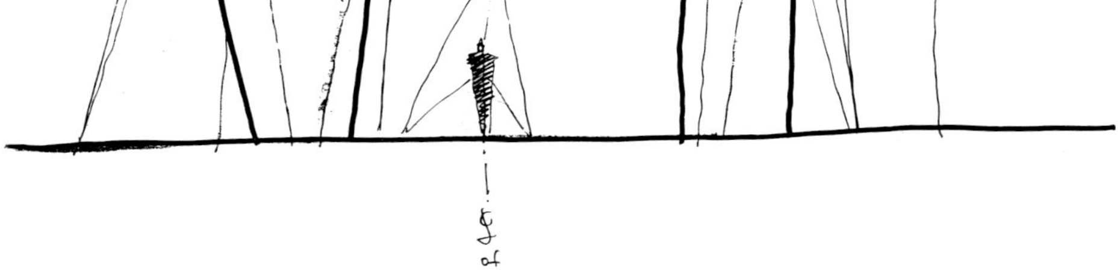

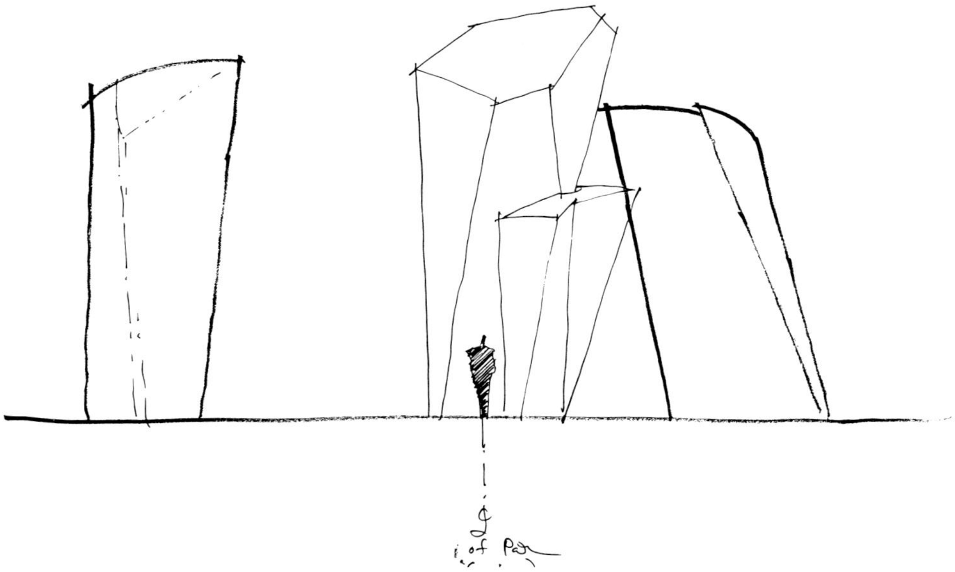

Possible surface finishes on a Prefabricated Fibreglass Reinforced Plastic (FRP) moulding range from polished high gloss to low lustre matt, from regular 'combing' to rough stone texture, and are a function of the mould from which they are made. The exterior surface usually consists of a polyester 'gel coat' formulated to be weather and stain resistant, and UV-stable. Sand-filled 'polymer concrete surfaces can be sand-blasted to look like real stone'. The Architectural Committee of the Composites Fabricators Association

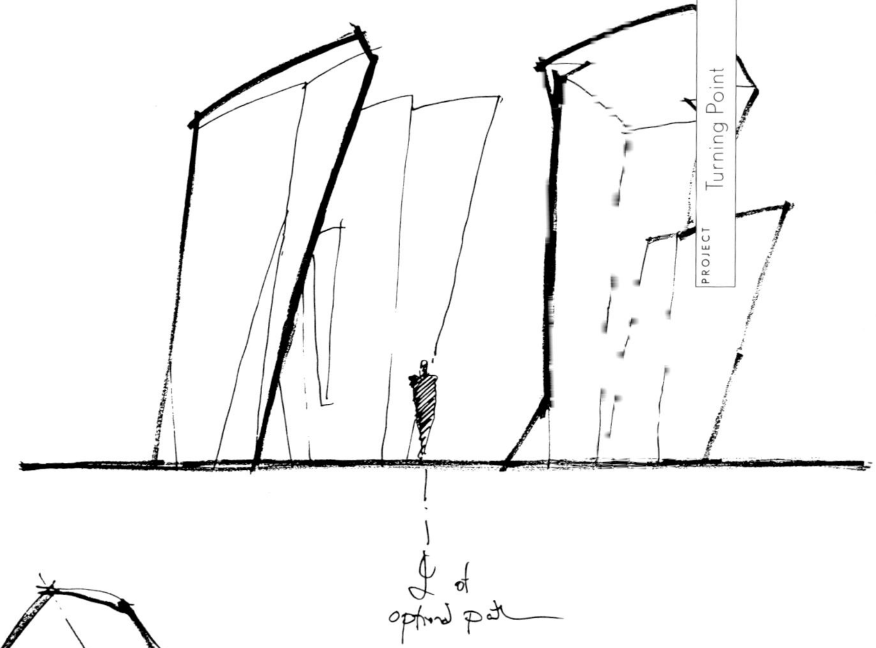

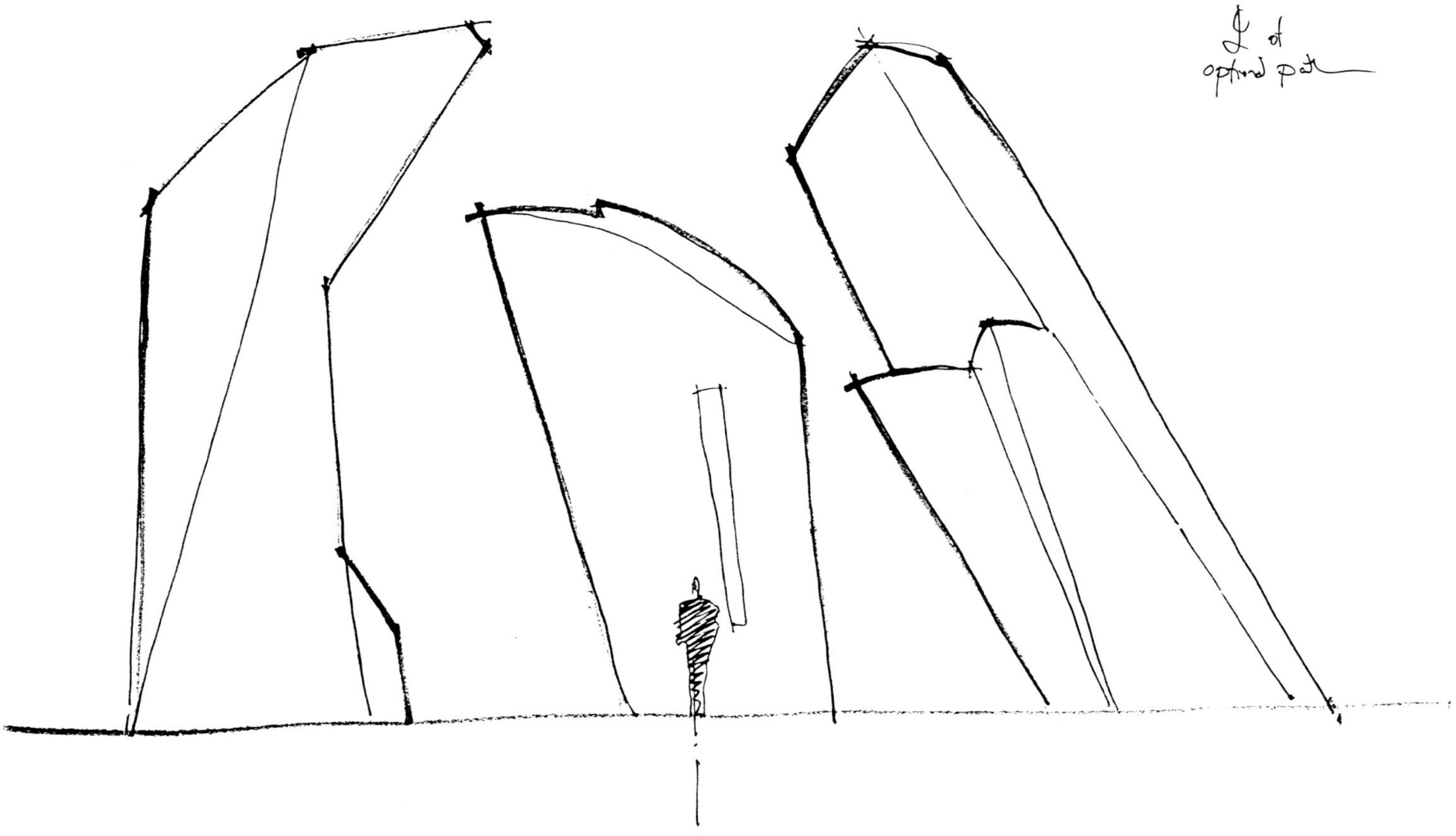

The angular and enclosing forms of the model recall the early work of the German Expressionists

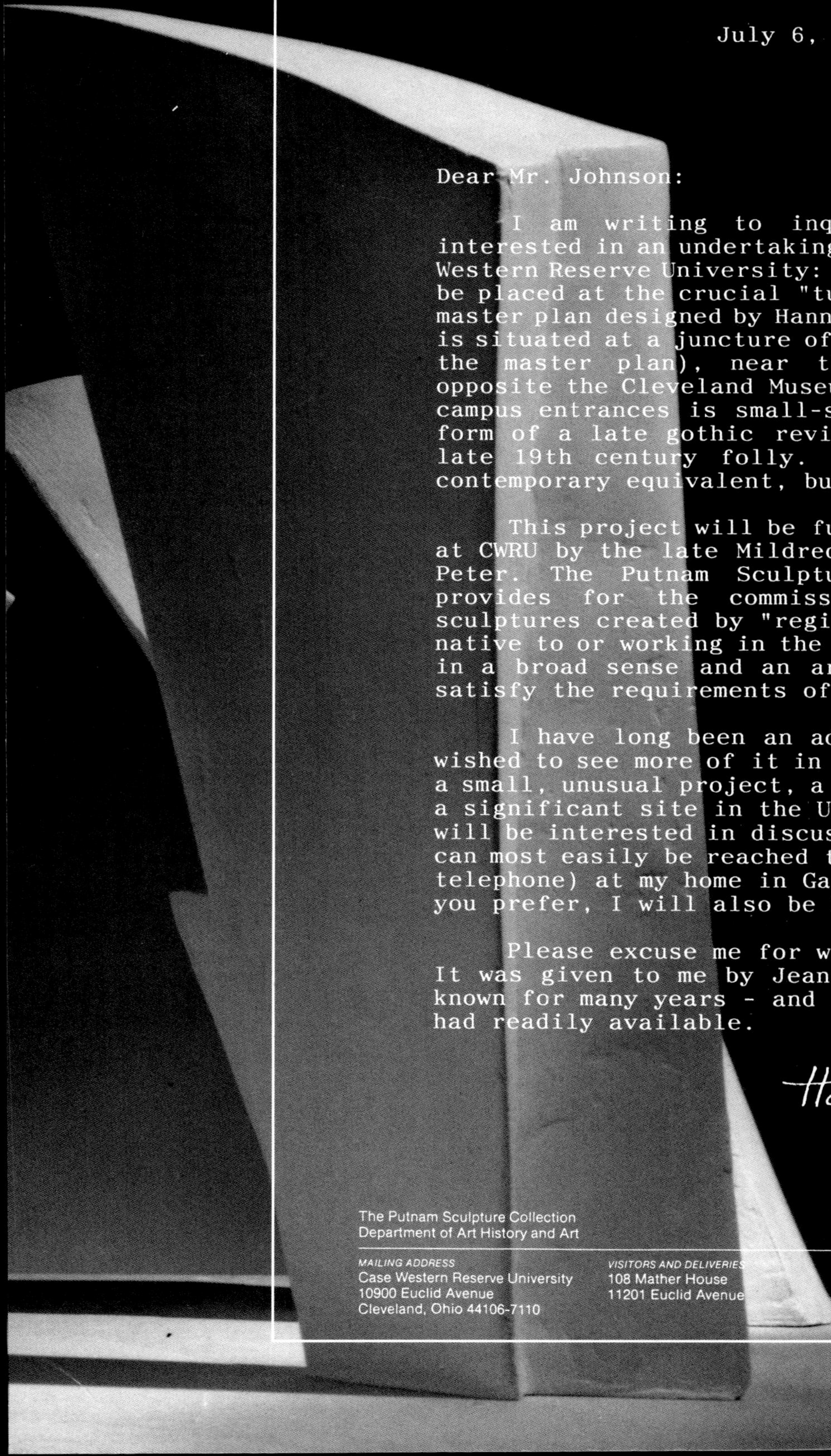

CASE WESTERN RESERVE UNIVERSITY

July 6, 1995

Dear Mr. Johnson:

I am writing to inquire whether you might be interested in an undertaking an unusual project for Case Western Reserve University: an architectural sculpture to be placed at the crucial "turning point" in a new campus master plan designed by Hanna/Olin Ltd. The turning point is situated at a juncture of the main path, (the spine of the master plan), near the new university library, opposite the Cleveland Museum of Art. One of the present campus entrances is small-scale stone structure in the form of a late gothic revival "Roman" arch, a kind of late 19th century folly. What I have in mind is a contemporary equivalent, but not necessarily an arch!

This project will be funded by an endowment created at CWRU by the late Mildred Andrews Putnam and her son Peter. The Putnam Sculpture Fund, which I direct, provides for the commissioning and acquisition of sculptures created by "regional" artists, i.e., artists native to or working in the region. Sculpture is defined in a broad sense and an architectural sculpture would satisfy the requirements of the endowment.

I have long been an admirer of your work and have wished to see more of it in Cleveland. What I propose is a small, unusual project, a work that would be placed at a significant site in the University Circle. I hope you will be interested in discussing this project further. I can most easily be reached this summer (by both mail and telephone) at my home in Gates Mills [redacted]. If you prefer, I will also be happy to come to New York.

Please excuse me for writing to your home address. It was given to me by Jeannette Dempsey - whom I have known for many years - and it was the only one that she had readily available.

Harvey Buchanan

The Putnam Sculpture Collection
Department of Art History and Art

MAILING ADDRESS
Case Western Reserve University
10900 Euclid Avenue
Cleveland, Ohio 44106-7110

VISITORS AND DELIVERIES
108 Mather House
11201 Euclid Avenue

Phone 216-368-4118
Fax 216-368-4681

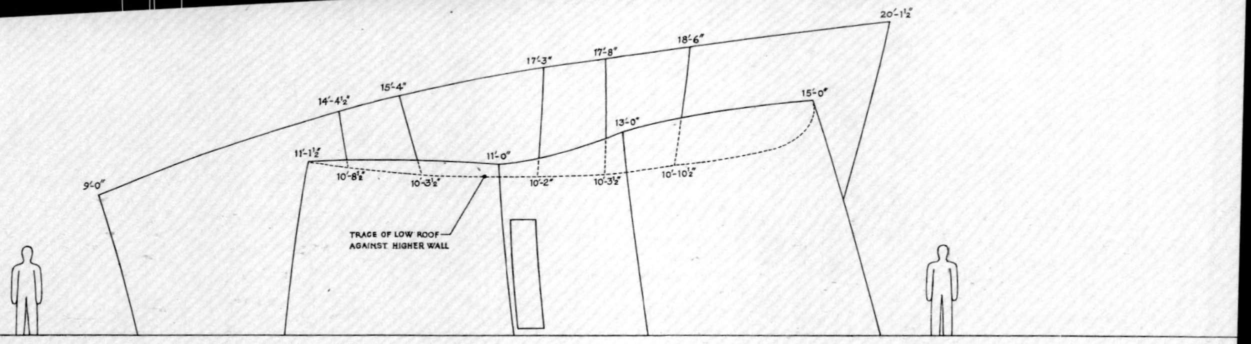

ELEVATION (A) 1/4" = 1'-0" • 4/18/94

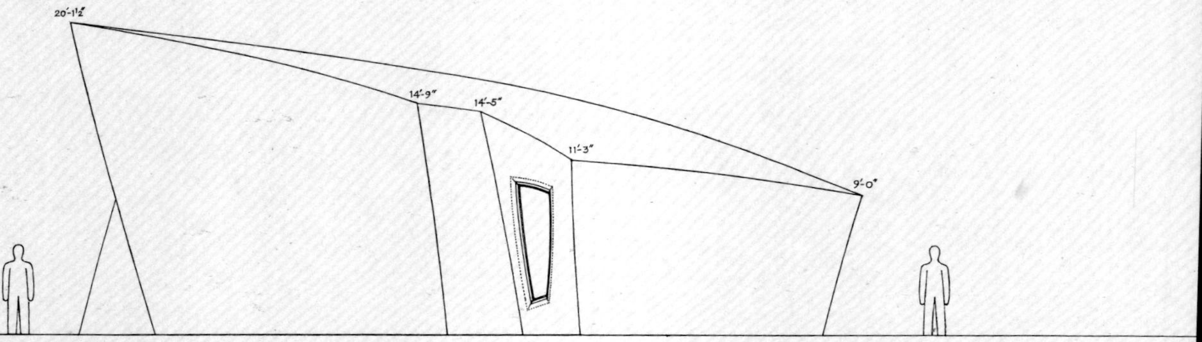

ELEVATION (B) 1/4" = 1'-0" • 5/25/94

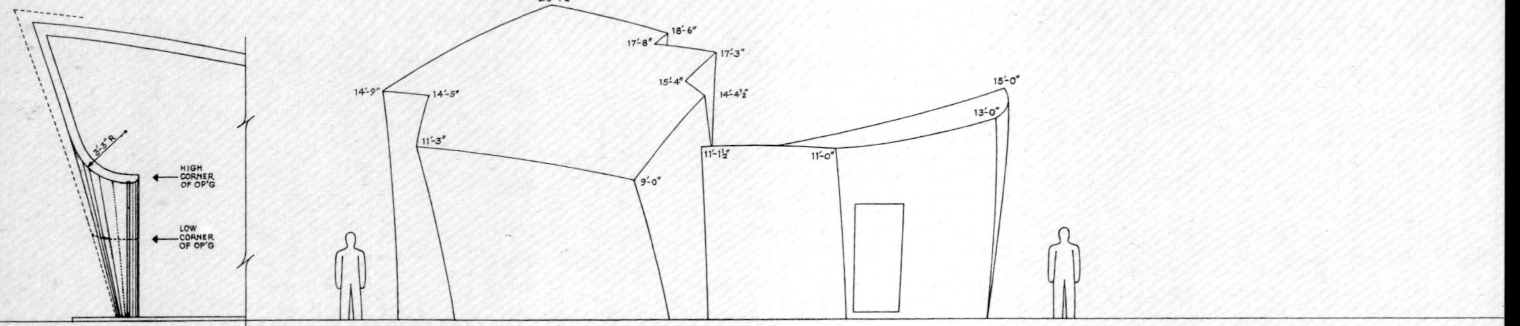

⇧ SECTION THROUGH ENTRANCE ⇩

ELEVATION (C) 1/4" = 1'-0" • 4/18/94

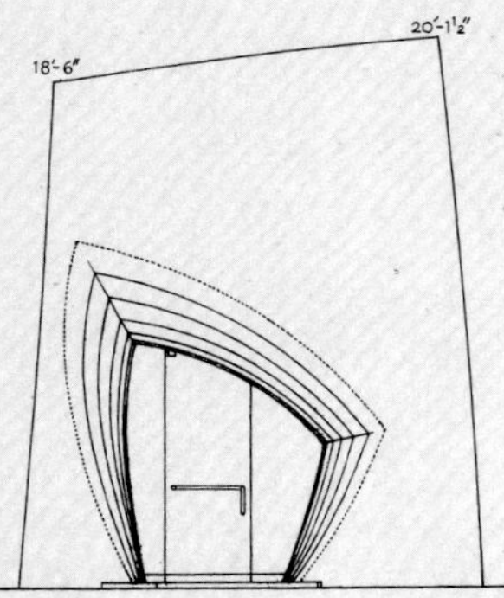

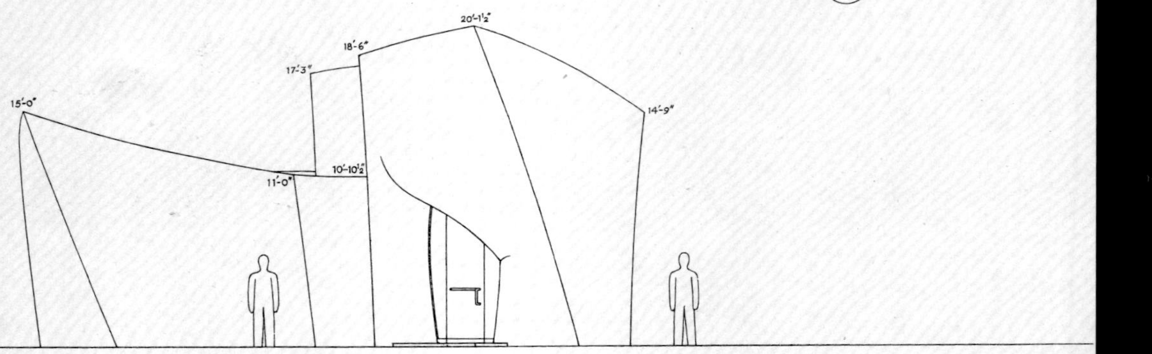

ELEVATION (E)

ELEVATION (D) 1/4" = 1'-0" • 5/10/94

GATE HOUSE NEW CANAAN, CONNECTICUT

PROJECT	Gate House
DESIGNER	Philip Johnson
ARCHITECT	John Manley
MANAGER	David Harrison

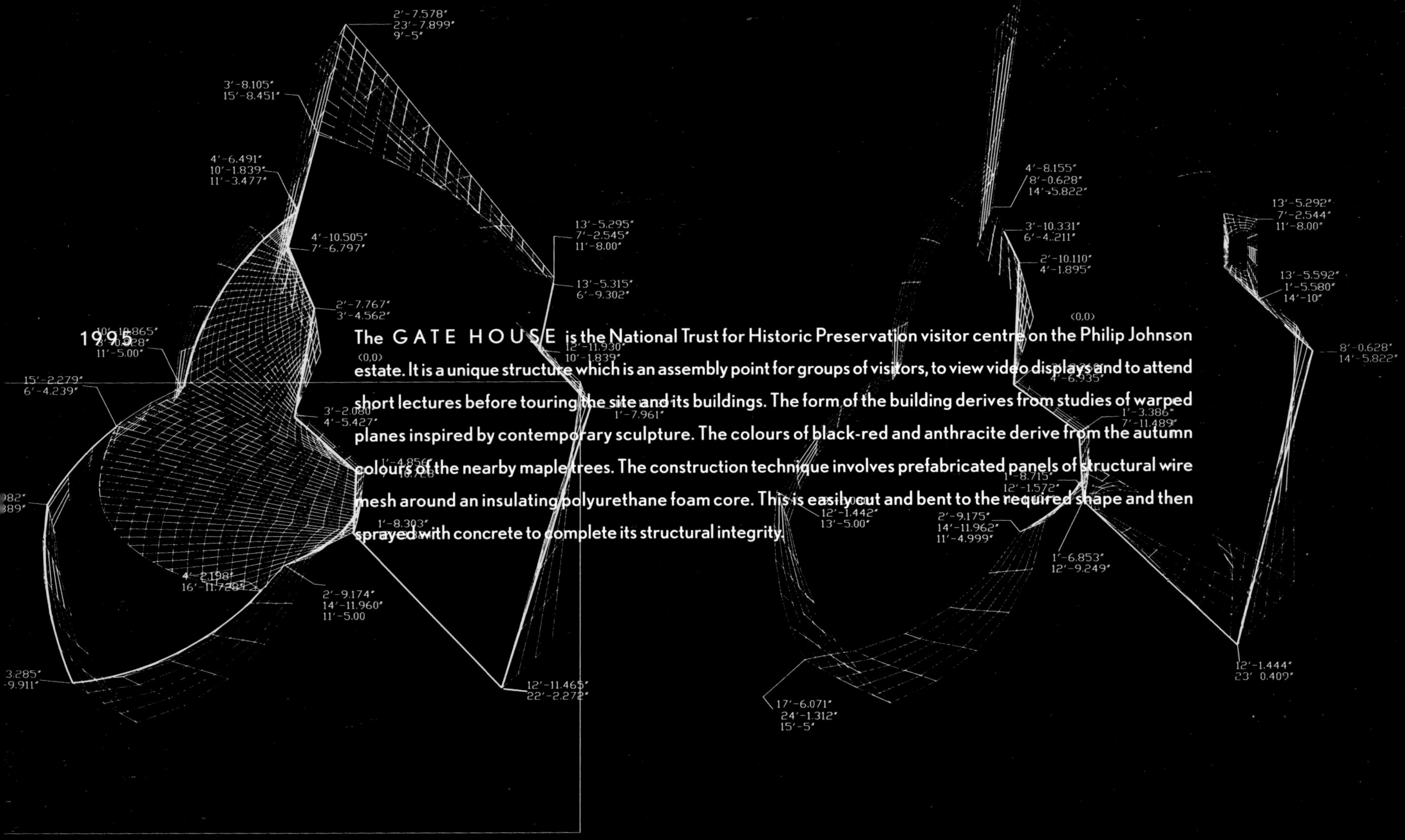

1995 The GATE HOUSE is the National Trust for Historic Preservation visitor centre on the Philip Johnson estate. It is a unique structure which is an assembly point for groups of visitors, to view video displays and to attend short lectures before touring the site and its buildings. The form of the building derives from studies of warped planes inspired by contemporary sculpture. The colours of black-red and anthracite derive from the autumn colours of the nearby maple trees. The construction technique involves prefabricated panels of structural wire mesh around an insulating polyurethane foam core. This is easily cut and bent to the required shape and then sprayed with concrete to complete its structural integrity.

Gate House

Israel A Seinuk, PC

When Philip Johnson created the last addition to his eclectic collection of architectural designs on his property in New Canaan, Connecticut, he chose an approach that was a radical departure from that of his famed Glass House. The new building would be a free-form collection of shapes inspired by a Frank Stella sculpture that mixes zigzag walls leaning in all directions, an arched and a dish-shaped roof, and door and window openings framed by inset curved surfaces.

The obvious question was: how do we build these? The answer lay in a method of construction that has been used internationally, mostly for fast erection, low-cost housing applications. This technique employs a manufactured wire mesh cage consisting of two sheets of welded wire mesh joined by diagonal wires. The cage is manufactured with a layer of polyurethane foam between the wire mesh sheets. In conventional applications, the panels are erected and then shotcreted. The final product is a continuously reinforced monolithic concrete building. The method was adapted for this particular application by taking advantage of the ability to mould that could be developed with these panels and the inherent plasticity of concrete. This was done by creating details that would allow the panels to be cut, joined, and curved to create the required free-form shapes. Using CAD, the design was transferred to full-scale templates which were erected as horizontal bands of wood on a central scaffold in such a way as to allow the contours to be followed by the interior of the erected panels. The panels were then cut and bent as required to fit the contours set by the templates. Since computer models and mock-ups never provide a full interpretation of a design, during and after panel erection, adjustments were made on different panels to vary the shape to suit the preferences of the architect.

Panel sizes were chosen to comply with structural and energy code requirements. The panels had the foam insulation custom-fabricated to a thickness of 76 millimetres and 117 millimetres to provide R values of 19 and 30 for the walls and roof respectively. The overall thickness, including the polyurethane, was 178 millimetres for the walls and 279 millimetres for the roof. These minimum values allow for the variations in overall thickness enforced by the contours.

This method enabled a unique degree of flexibility in the placement of openings for windows and doors. In each case, an outline of the door or window opening was spray-painted on to the erected panels and repeatedly moved until the architect was finally satisfied with the location. The openings were then cut in place. One of these door openings was subsequently found to be unnecessary, and was repanelled, and the reinforcement spliced to restore its continuity. Today it is impossible to identify the location of the cut.

Where required, the panels were reinforced with conventional reinforcing bars and welded wire mesh. Joints between panels and between the panels and the foundations were made with a mix of reinforcing bars and factory supplied splice meshes. Shotcreting used the wet mix process, which was preferred because it provides better control over the water content of the mix. The strength of the mix was set at 4000 psi.

For the walls, the shotcrete was applied in two layers. The first layer was placed between the foam and the wire mesh and then struck off. This layer stiffened the assemblage of panels to allow for the removal of much of the horizontal templates and scaffolding. The second layer provided the finished thickness of the wall and the required cover for the reinforcement. The shotcreting of the underside of the roof was similar to the walls. The concrete on the top of the roof was applied in one layer. Fine contouring and shaping of surfaces and corners was achieved with a high density mortar mix.

The finished building is a testament to the versatility of reinforced concrete when its plasticity is employed to its fullest extent. The techniques used have produced a building of unique sculptural qualities, a building that provides singular interior spaces and an extremely pleasing visual signature.

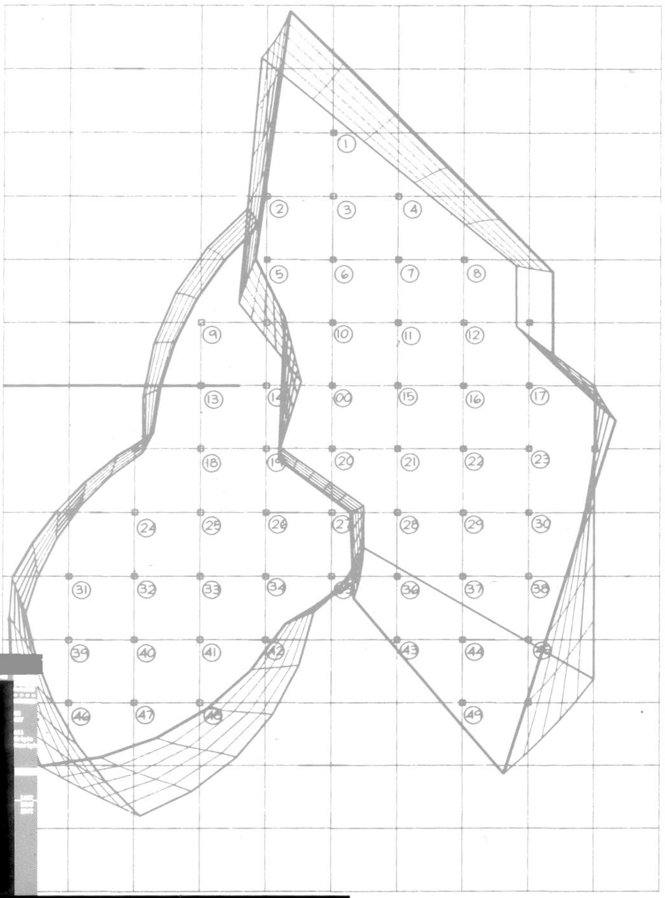

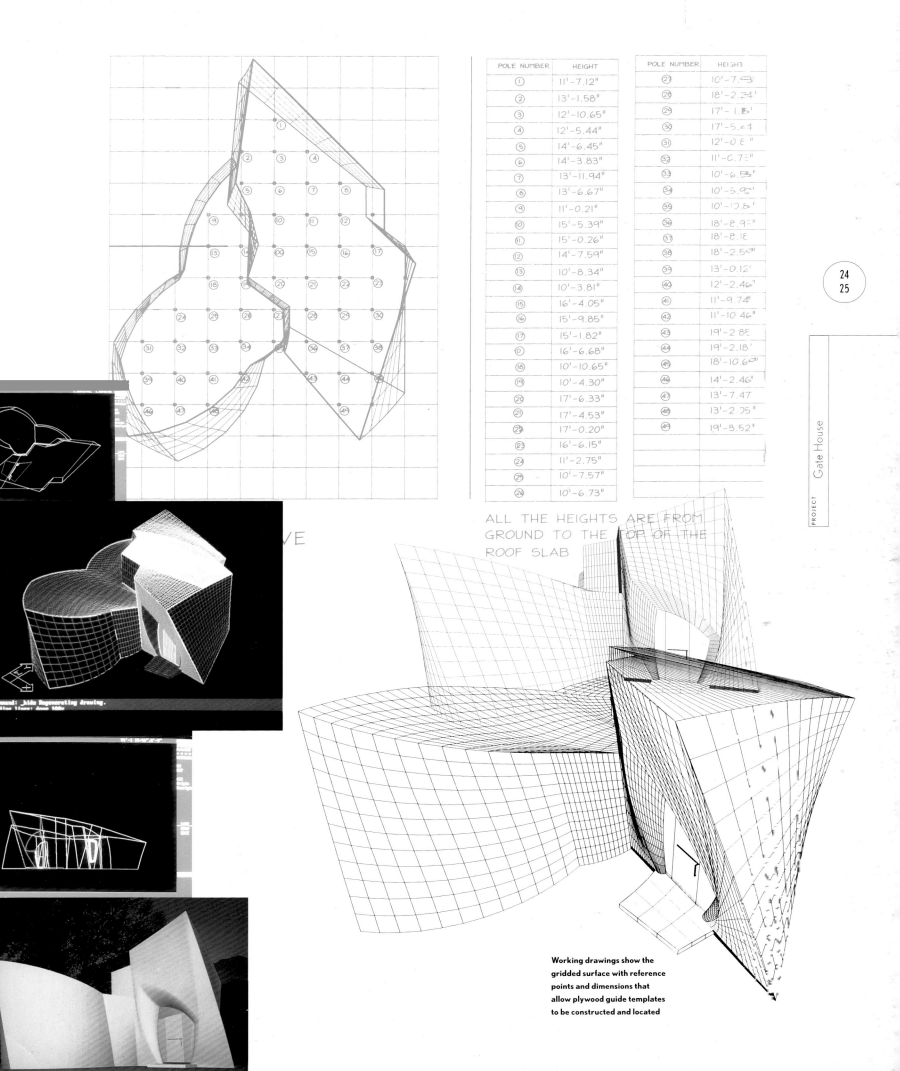

POLE NUMBER	HEIGHT	POLE NUMBER	HEIGHT
1	11'-7.12"	27	10'-7.[illegible]
2	13'-1.58"	28	18'-2.34'
3	12'-10.65"	29	17'-1.[illegible]'
4	12'-5.44"	30	17'-5.[illegible]
5	14'-6.45"	31	12'-0.8 "
6	14'-3.83"	32	11'-0.7[illegible]"
7	13'-11.94"	33	10'-6.5[illegible]'
8	13'-6.67"	34	10'-5.9[illegible]'
9	11'-0.21"	35	10'-10.8[illegible]'
10	15'-5.39"	36	18'-8.9[illegible]"
11	15'-0.26"	37	18'-8.18
12	14'-7.59"	38	18'-2.5[illegible]"
13	10'-8.34"	39	13'-0.12'
14	10'-3.81"	40	12'-2.46'
15	16'-4.05"	41	11'-9.74"
16	15'-9.85"	42	11'-10 46"
17	15'-1.82"	43	19'-2 85
0	16'-6.68"	44	19'-2.18'
18	10'-10.65"	45	18'-10.6[illegible]"
19	10'-4.30"	46	14'-2.46"
20	17'-6.33"	47	13'-7.47
21	17'-4.53"	48	13'-2.05"
22	17'-0.20"	49	19'-8.52"
23	16'-6.15"		
24	11'-2.75"		
25	10'-7.57"		
26	10'-6.73"		

ALL THE HEIGHTS ARE FROM GROUND TO THE TOP OF THE ROOF SLAB

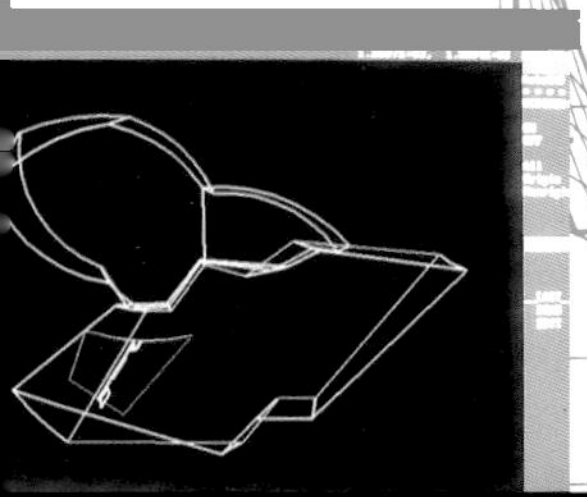

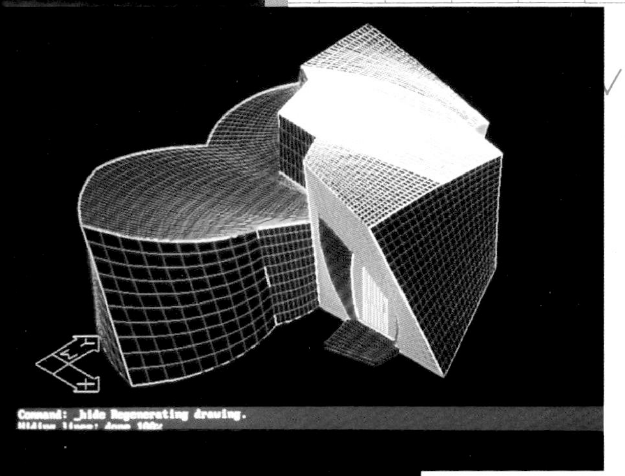

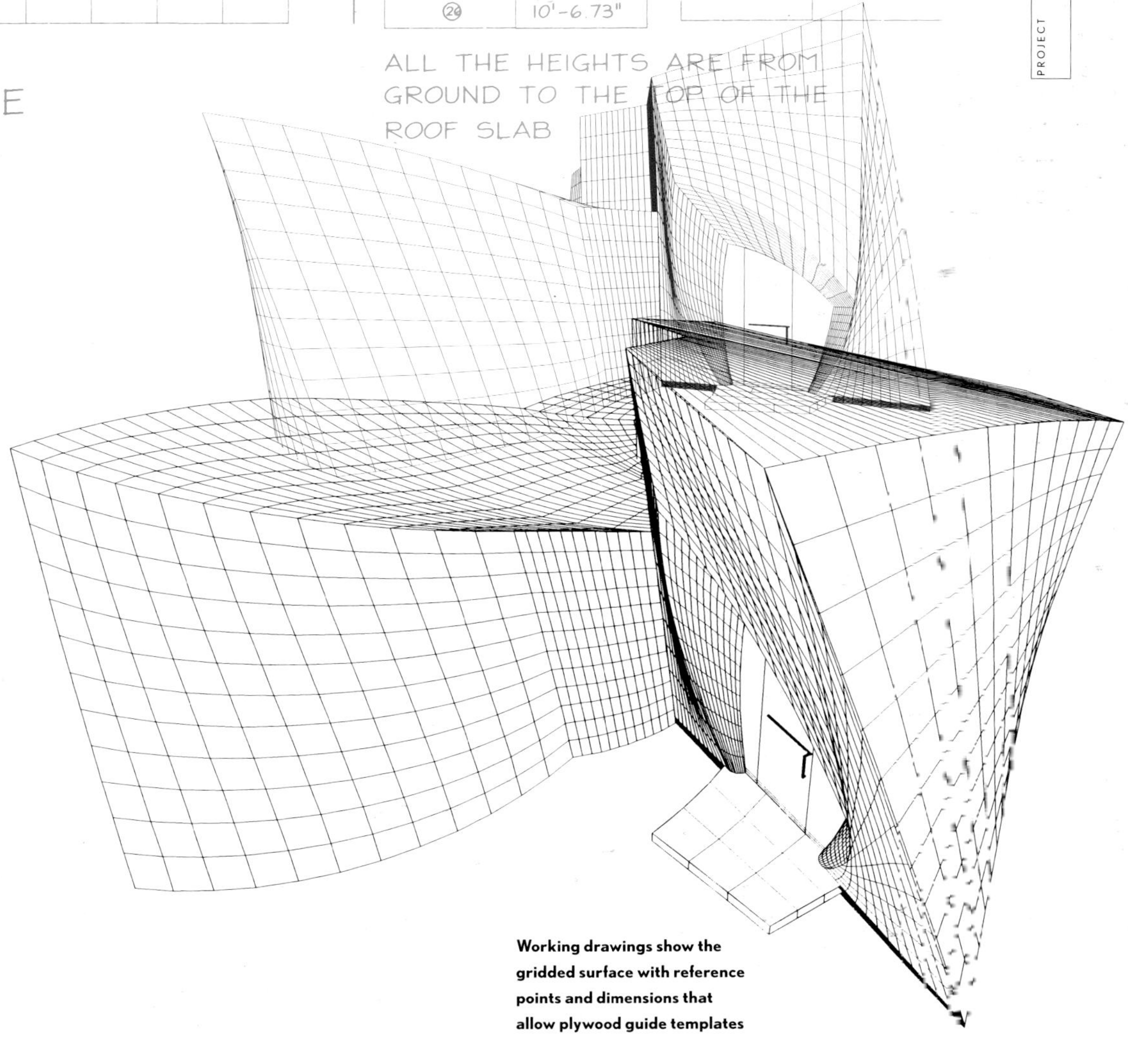

Working drawings show the gridded surface with reference points and dimensions that allow plywood guide templates to be constructed and located

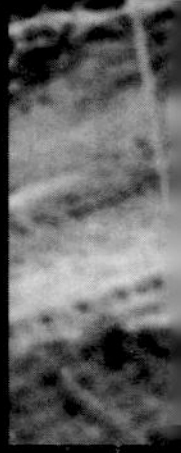

Early perspective study of Gate House and photograph of site excavation and surveyed 'points' with chalk marks locating walls

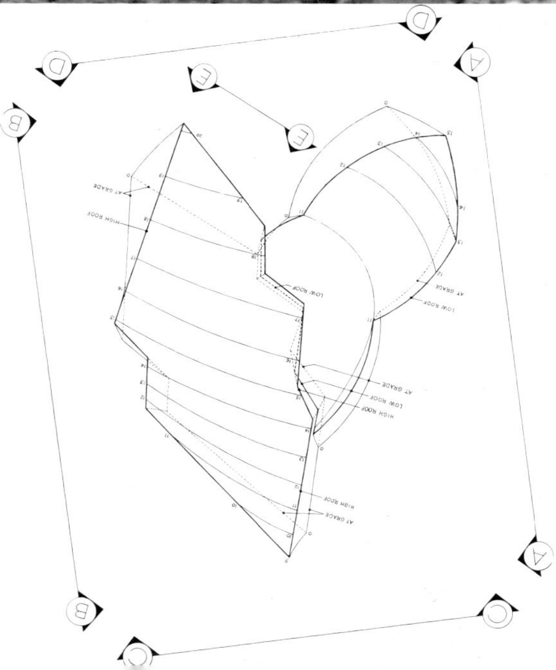

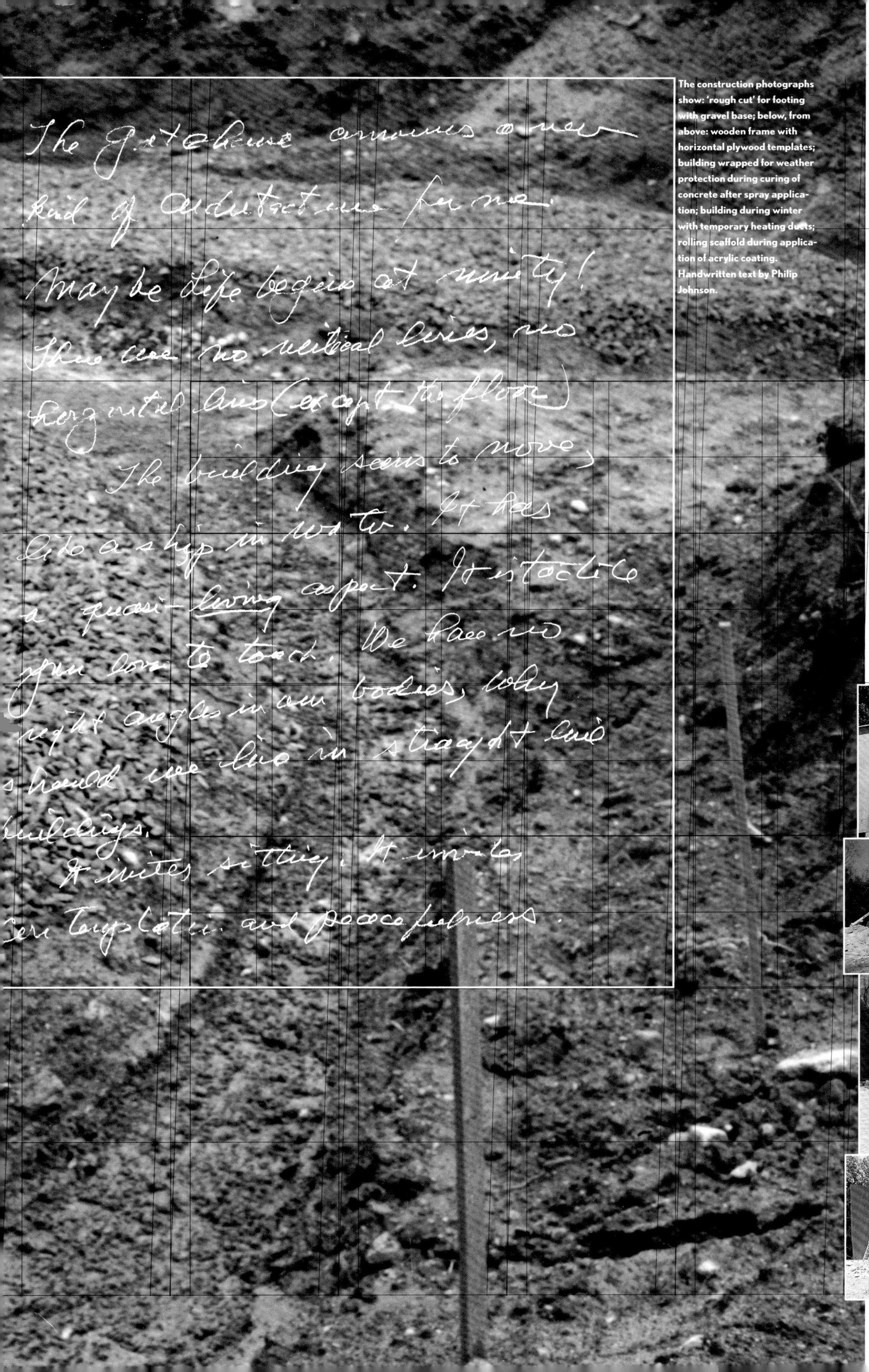
The Gatehouse announces a new
kind of architecture for me.
Maybe life begins at ninety!
There are no vertical lines, no
horizontal lines (except the floor)
The building seems to move,
like a ship in water. It has
a quasi-living aspect. It is tactile
you love to touch. We have no
right angles in our bodies, why
should we live in straight line
buildings.
It invites sitting. It invites
contemplation and peacefulness.

The construction photographs show: 'rough cut' for footing with gravel base; below, from above: wooden frame with horizontal plywood templates; building wrapped for weather protection during curing of concrete after spray application; building during winter with temporary heating ducts; rolling scaffold during application of acrylic coating. Handwritten text by Philip Johnson.

Construction photographs show sequence of exterior assembly and finishing from above left, anti-clockwise: horizontal plywood guide templates located and supported by wood framing; assembly of panels complete on left side; assembly of panels complete on building; large entry opening cut out and corners reinforced by weaving in extra bars; concrete finish applied with plywood formwork at cornice as pour stops for roof; building cleaned and prepared for final finish coat and colour

BERLIN

Model of elevation along
Friedrichstrasse in Berlin Mitte

ALTERNATIVE

BERLIN, GERMANY

PROJECT Berlin Alternative
DESIGNER Philip Johnson
MANAGER John Manley
ASSOCIATE ARCHITECTS Pysall, Stahrenberg & Partners

1993

BERLIN ALTERNATIVE was developed in reaction to the present Berlin Government requirements to rebuild the Friedrichstrasse area following eighteenth-century urban design guidelines. It presents a scheme whose southern 'prow' faces the former Checkpoint Charlie site on Friedrichstrasse. This scheme has not been limited by building height requirements or zoning setbacks in the hope of stimulating discussion on other urban strategies besides the current nostalgia. Its inspiration is the German Expressionist movement in the twenties, shaped in Berlin by architects as diverse as Mendelsohn, Taut, Poelzig, Finsterlin and the early Mies van der Rohe. It thus connects to a tradition of a specific Berlin spirit projecting a future of anti-Platonic rules and theories.

Philip Johnson

June 13, 1993

Berlin's Last Chance - Schinkel, Messel, Mies van der Rohe - Now What?

I am interested only in the art of architecture. Even the art of painting leaves me less than ecstatic, perhaps with few exceptions - Caspar David Friedrich, Paul Klee, Piero della Francesca. Politics interest me only in so far as it fosters or impedes the production of architectural beauty. For example, I loathe Hitler but love Friedrich Wilhelm IV: bad client, good client.

Then, of course, comes the supreme expression of architectural art - Städtebau: I love Sienna, Priene, the Rome of Sixtus, the squares of London, the gardens of Le Notre's Vaux-le-Vicomte or the romantic gardens at Wörlitz.

Then I have my hates: all the city plans of Le Corbusier and Hilberseimer. In fact, I know of no plans of the International Style, even Taut's Hufeisenseidlung or Gropius' Siemensstadt, that I can bear. How very sad that, in the end, the Modernists were brilliant builders but abysmal planners. Doubly sad for me because much of my lifetime was spent promoting Modern architecture, preaching the beauties of buildings by such geniuses as Le Corbusier and Mies.

Which brings me to the city of Berlin. As a foreigner, I have had three separate and distinct experiences here: first, at the end of the Weimar days, when I spent the better part of three years here; the second was in the fifties, when Berlin was unbearably sad; the third is this year, as I take a small part in the rebirth of Berlin. I have been commissioned to build on historic ground in the Friedrichstadt - an assignment which I take extremely seriously.

Of these three trips to Berlin, I must admit I most enjoyed the first. Only Julius Posener can really remember these days as well as I do. For me it was more of a surprise and pleasure than it ever could have been for a native Berliner. At the time, in the United States, there was no ‘Modern’ culture. There was no Klee, no Kandinsky, no Bauhaus, no Mies van der Rohe, no Taut, no Mendelsohn, no Modern dance, no Wigman, Moholy-Nagy, no Piscator for theatre design. I am only sorry that other cultural fields were closed to me. My bad German did not allow me to understand the poetry, for example. Nevertheless, the air we breathed, the people that we came to know, the restaurants, the Kurfürstendamm, the sex life were all new, all thrilling to a young American. The world was being created here in Berlin. The beer was better, the friendliness toward strangers unequalled. Nowhere in the world were we Americans received with such welcome.

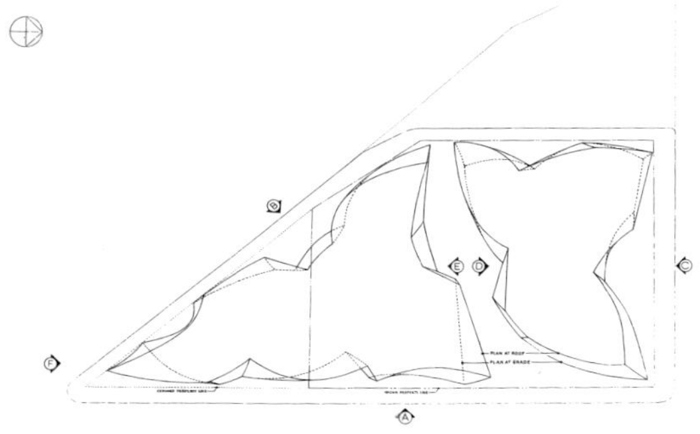

FLOOR AND ROOF PLANS

In my intoxication with Berlin's modern life, I completely missed the underlying political difficulties that were developing. I knew no outspoken Communists or outspoken Nazis, though maybe they just did not tell me. I floated on the wonders of the new culture and, most of all, the new architecture.

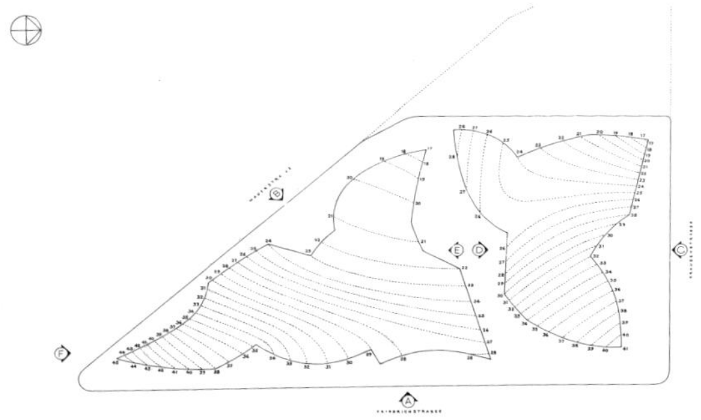

ROOF CONTOURS
1:500 · APRIL 8,1993

I spent a great deal of my time and energy in those years in Potsdam and on the architecture of romantic classicism in the company of Schinkel, Persius and their followers. Klein Glienicke and Charlottenhof today remain my favourite building groups.

Of the Städtebau of Berlin however, I knew little. When I arrived I got off the train from the West at the Friedrichstrasse Bahnhof and found a hotel across the street. I was surprised to find the so-called Stadtmitte empty of people. It was some time before I found the Kurfürstendamm. The discovery of two city centres was disorienting and perplexing, which in a way, Berlin still is. Unification is going to take a long time and many milliards of marks plus a lot of luck. On the other hand, it is the key experiment for the future of the West.

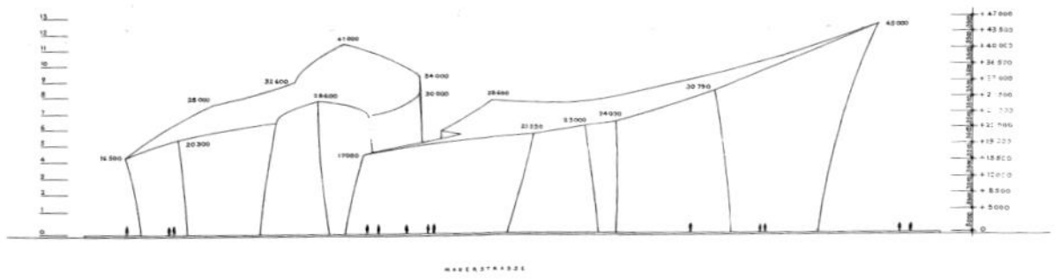

ELEVATION (B)

Though the plan of Berlin was a bit perplexing, the *architecture* that I found here was not. Schinkel's genius was the embodiment of clarity. His concept of city planning is shown best in the engraving of a view from the balcony of the Altes Museum looking toward the Schloss and the Friedrich-Werdersche-Kirche across the Lustgarten. Each building is very different from the other, as the Friedrich-Werdersche-Kirche, the Bauakademie, the project for the State Library and the Kaufhaus show. They are autonomous self-contained images, remotely related, just the opposite of the unified aspect, for example, of the two eighteenth-century Baroque squares at Nancy.

We can compare the eighteenth-century Schloss in Potsdam with its several adjoining buildings to Schinkel's arrangement across the Sanssouci park of the Charlottenhof with its nearby building the Hofgärtnerei. In the latter scheme each building is in a different 'style' of architecture, if you will, and placed at an *ad hoc* angle with respect to the other, though both face the park of Sanssouci.

This use of autonomous structures related loosely to other buildings is the kind of city planning that might work today. Schinkel's buildings fit into any pre-existing city. The great Schinkel fits better into Berlin's building today, even with the Hansaviertel or the Zeilenbau of Modern architecture.

In truth, however, my first visit concerned itself less with the city than with the Modern Movement as such. The twenties were the days of utopias, the days when many were convinced of the end of monumentality, symbolic, emotional or spiritual architecture. Housing for the masses seemed the main goal of Modern architecture. Socialism was attainable. Karl-Marx-Hof in Vienna, Römerstadt in Frankfurt were the ideal.

(3)

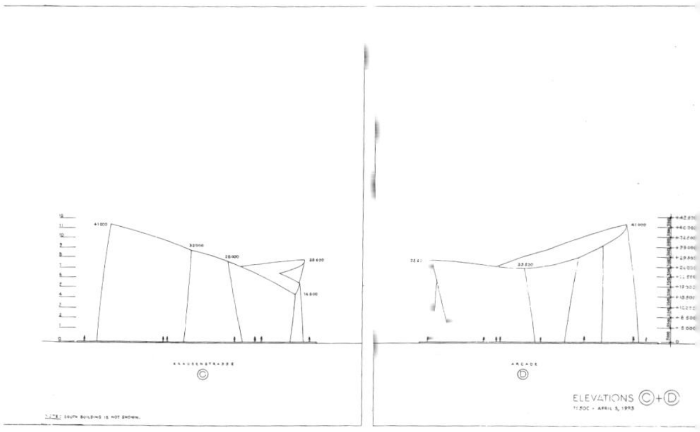

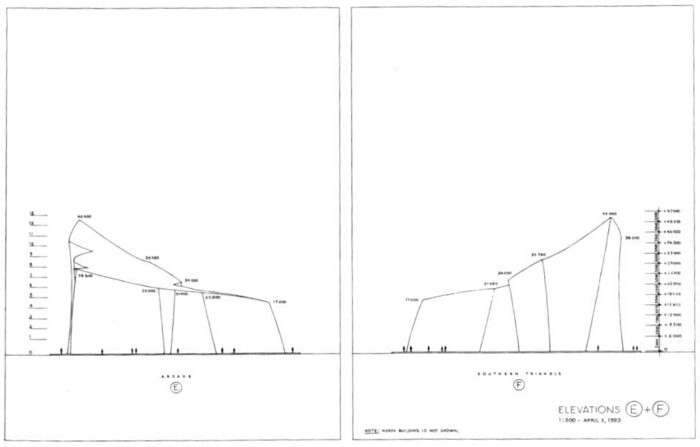

Study sketches of various elevations in the design process

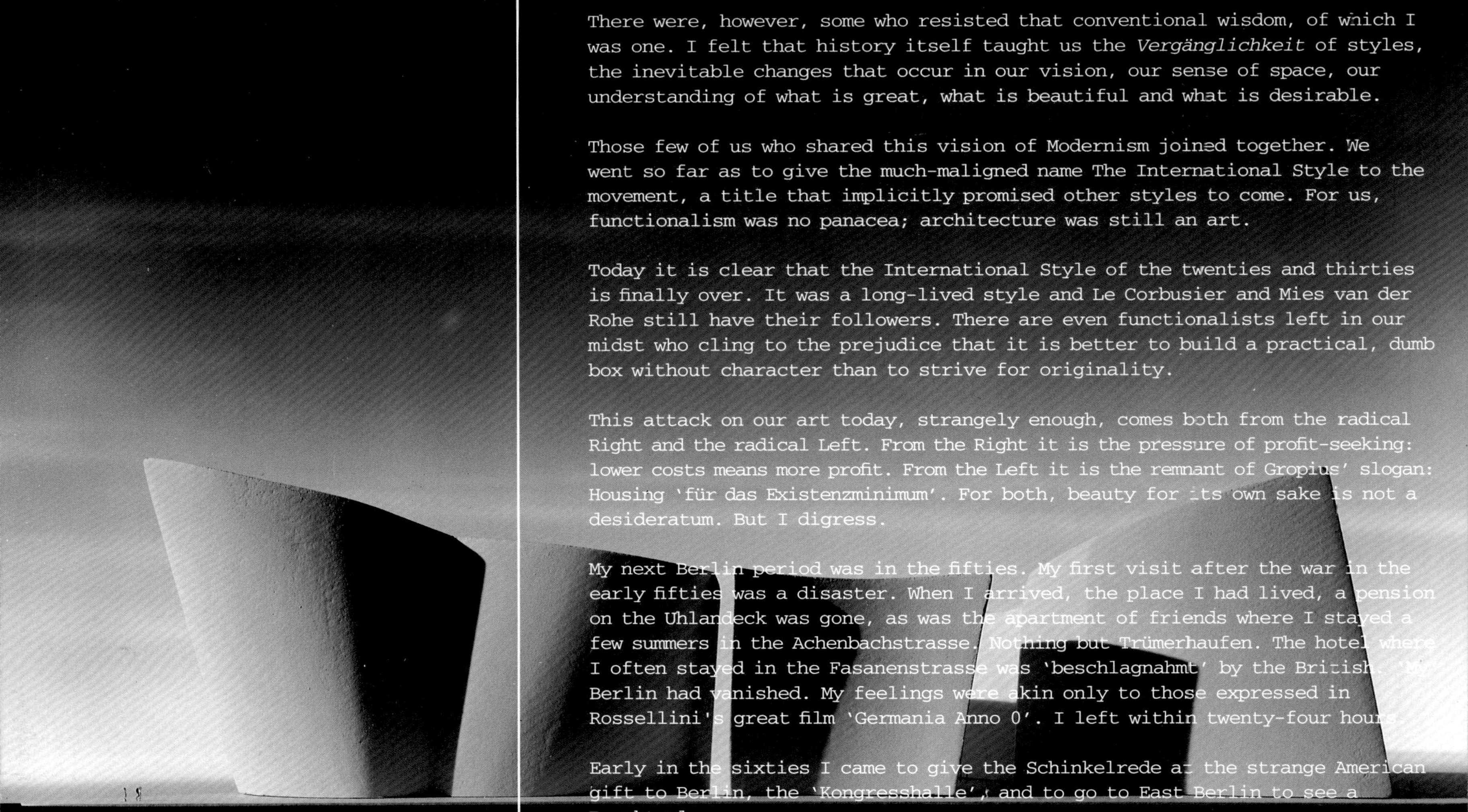

There were, however, some who resisted that conventional wisdom, of which I was one. I felt that history itself taught us the *Vergänglichkeit* of styles, the inevitable changes that occur in our vision, our sense of space, our understanding of what is great, what is beautiful and what is desirable.

Those few of us who shared this vision of Modernism joined together. We went so far as to give the much-maligned name The International Style to the movement, a title that implicitly promised other styles to come. For us, functionalism was no panacea; architecture was still an art.

Today it is clear that the International Style of the twenties and thirties is finally over. It was a long-lived style and Le Corbusier and Mies van der Rohe still have their followers. There are even functionalists left in our midst who cling to the prejudice that it is better to build a practical, dumb box without character than to strive for originality.

This attack on our art today, strangely enough, comes both from the radical Right and the radical Left. From the Right it is the pressure of profit-seeking: lower costs means more profit. From the Left it is the remnant of Gropius' slogan: Housing 'für das Existenzminimum'. For both, beauty for its own sake is not a desideratum. But I digress.

My next Berlin period was in the fifties. My first visit after the war in the early fifties was a disaster. When I arrived, the place I had lived, a pension on the Uhlandeck was gone, as was the apartment of friends where I stayed a few summers in the Achenbachstrasse. Nothing but Trümerhaufen. The hotel where I often stayed in the Fasanenstrasse was 'beschlagnahmt' by the British. 'My' Berlin had vanished. My feelings were akin only to those expressed in Rossellini's great film 'Germania Anno 0'. I left within twenty-four hours.

Early in the sixties I came to give the Schinkelrede at the strange American gift to Berlin, the 'Kongresshalle', and to go to East Berlin to see a Brecht play.

It was a good opportunity to see what a great city would do in order to recreate itself. Also, it was easy to compare the East and the West at work. My impression was not favourable to the West. True, new streets were built, Autobahnen even, complete with underpasses and overpasses. The Kempinski was still there for foreigners. The Kurfürstendamm existed. But, I thought, what new buildings? The only public building was Hugh Stubbins' 'pregnant oyster', the Kongresshalle. Where was the symbolic building of the renewed Germany?

Then I went looking in the East. The Schinkel buildings were there, even the Bauakademie, which later was shamefully torn down. The Neue Wache was restored, the Altes Museum beautifully kept up (the addition of a glass partition wall came much, much later). Even the Stadtschloss had not yet disappeared.

(4)

Photographs of the models of all four elevations presented at the end of Philip Johnson's June 1993 lecture, Berlin, Germany

Then further east, I found public monuments to please all of us unreconstructed lovers of symbolic monumentality: first the great memorial to the Russian dead where the beautiful granite work and the glorious full-grown trees impressed and moved me in their stark contrast to the destruction of the rest of the city.

Henselmann's Stalinallee however was real city planning in the grand manner. His designs in no way tended toward the modern but they did make me realise: here is a culture with architectural ambitions. Let me assure you I was never a Communist sympathiser. I just wished that our side, the West, had the architectural will both to grieve our war losses and to celebrate a hopeful future.

To me it was also a disappointment that the West had not taken care of Schinkel's work. For example, I found the little pavilion at Glienicke derelict. This small building had a great influence on Mies' work as well as on my own. West Berlin was still depressing ten years after the war and East Berlin had not yet taken on the sadness of later Communism.

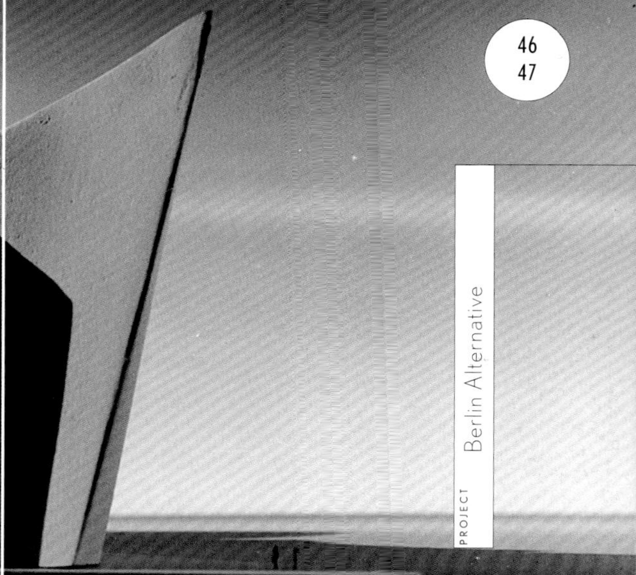

Let us talk of my third sojourn in Berlin. Berlin is one city again, hopes are high for a bright economic future, competitions proliferate; Potsdamer Platz, Reichstag, Friedrichstrasse and Spreebogen. Bahnhof area, Friedrichstadt and more.

But what aesthetic authority governs the selection process? Whose decision on architectural city planning are we to follow? We hear enough about high-rise versus low-rise. We hear about history. We have heard how in the last generation Le Corbusier and Scharoun proposed plans that ran counter to the spirit of Berlin. Therefore, along with the present rejection of their very [illegible] comes the question, what then?

I think quite naturally of the Friedrichstadt because it is where I am working right now. It is also the most sensitive central part of all Berlin, and it is still a 'tabula rasa'. Should Berlin become a Warsaw and rebuild copies of the old Friedrichstadt? I think not. Should we take away the streets and go back to Gropius and build more Zeilenbau? Or should we opt for a new solution: a Coop Himmelblau? a Zaha Hadid? a Daniel Libeskind? Common wisdom is that these designers do not understand the city's history and cannot subordinate their arrogant individualism. Parenthetically, I sympathise with the young people. They should have a chance.

Would it help perhaps if the authorities forbade foreign architects? There are many arguments for such a course. Who better than the Germans, who live the history of their city, to design their own capital? However sensible this argument might at first sound, such xenophobia cannot be tolerated in today's world, and in Berlin of all places.

(5)

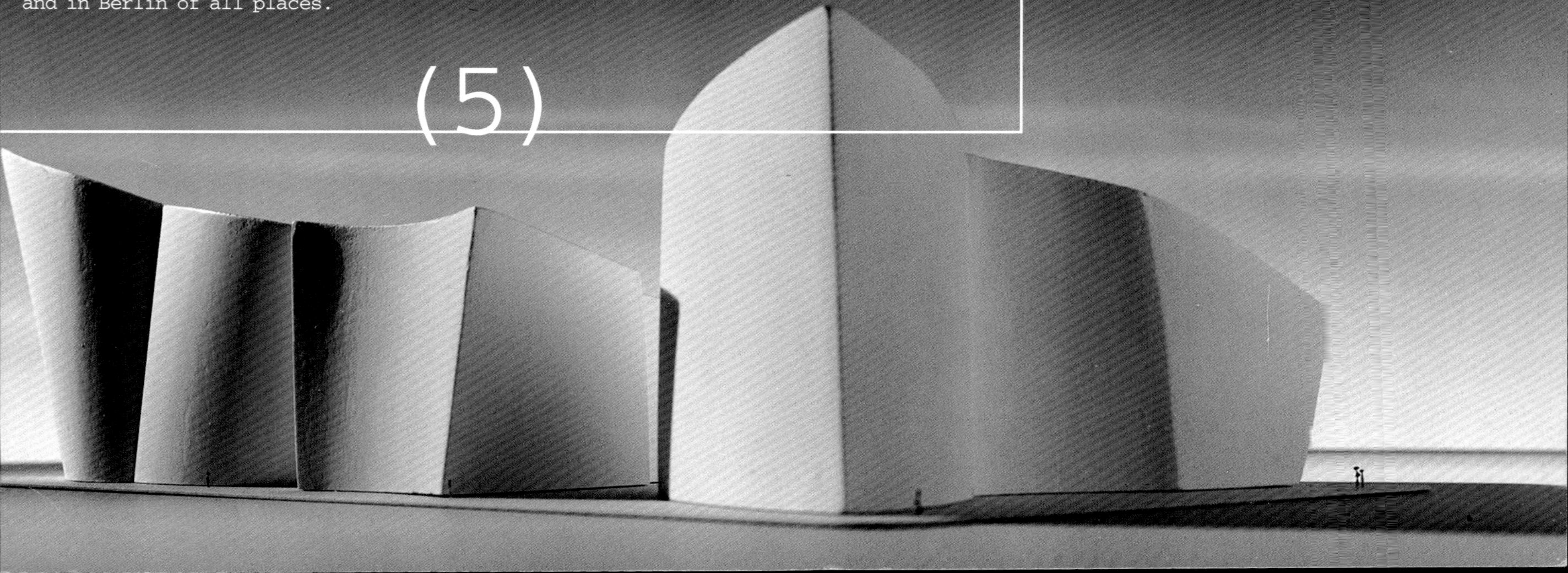

(6)

(7)

Should we simply bide our time, and wait for a Bernini, a Michelangelo, a Weinbrenner, Le Notre or in the last hope a Haussman or a Daniel Burnham to emerge? Or perhaps we need a patron like a Louis or a Sixtus to tell the geniuses what to do. No such patron seems to be on the horizon, nor would we obey any longer such a solitary heroic voice.

It occurs to me, however, to suggest that we take a second look at the career of the man I consider to have been Berlin's greatest architectural city planner – Schinkel.

There are problems with Schinkel as a model. Until recently, he has been considered a painter, an architect, a panorama designer, a state official who knew his politics, but has been denigrated as a city planner, even by an early enthusiast like me. His buildings look isolated, freestanding, and not integrated into a completed Stadtbild. His ability to recreate a great centre of a city – Berlin – and at the same time to preserve and harmonise the existing building pattern has been overlooked.

First he was able to work within the existing city plan. At the Brandenburger Tor he anchored the Pariser Platz with the Florentine Palais Redern. His idea for ending the extension of the Wilhelmstrasse by extending the building over the street emphasises the continuity of the Linden.

Schinkel's greatest planning achievement however, was the sequence of spaces at the Lustgarten complex with its connection to the Werderscher Markt. It is a sequence that challenges the greatest Baroque plans. He was able to work into the design all existing monuments. He even kept unimportant existing buildings. No city planner up to Schinkel ever succeeded in this process. In the Lustgarten he honoured the Domkirche, the Zeughaus, the royal palace, the commercial area of the Packhof and in addition built the greatest architectural masterpieces of the century to emphasise and decorate the sequence: the Altes Museum, the Werdersche-Kirche, the Bauakademie and the bridge connecting the Spree Island and even an enormous fountain on the axis of the Linden. What the Linden axis does to the Lustgarten is the key to the whole asymmetric twist that he has given to this old sector.Never in city planning has a strong processional like the Linden ended in an enclosed square that is located off-axis to such a degree. Schinkel's fountain would have emphasised this in an extremely modern way.

King Friedrich Wilhelm III refused the fountain; the Werderscher Markt project also was unrealised. It was an Italianate square with a church and a separate campanile. Also on the square were the Alte Münz building and the new Bauakademie by Schinkel. A new street broke through to the east of the French Street and continued on into the Schloss Platz. The lynch pin was the Bauakademie facing both ways: the Lustgarten to the north and the Werderscher Markt to the south.

The Lustgarten itself would have been an enclosed square, not a throughway; the royal palace on the south, the Domkirche with Schinkel's portico on the east, the Altes Museum by Schinkel on the north then a slight offset for the entrance pavilion of the Packhof also by Schinkel. On the west the Kupfergraben dominated by the eighteenth-century Zeughaus. South of that, the Bauakademie.

This is a city plan to rival any capital in the world: a large square, a small intimate square, a baroque *allée*, all very loosely connected. Old buildings and new, mixed and of different styles. Schinkel's great invention was *intervention*, a word much used by city planners faced with existing fabrics into which to insert more designs. My young theorist friends today speak of a 'new cohesiveness' in planning. By that I believe they mean plans in which disparate elements – old and new – enter into loose organisations. It seems to me that Schinkel achieved precisely that effect in his Lustgarten scheme.

The days of baroque splendour are over. There remains only 'Intervention'. Genius will know how to use it. Schinkel shows the way with his odd juxtaposition, his sometimes quirky sequences, but also with his startling ability to unify whole designs.

To my disappointment, the present government of Berlin has chosen a different path. It is, thank goodness, not the path of Modern architecture, the point buildings and row housing of Gropius or Hilberseimer, or the *grandezza* of a Baron Haussmann with his network of neo-baroque streets plowing up the old: nor

A Berlin Alternative

Leslie E Robertson,
Leslie E Robertson Associates, Engineers

This proposed multi-storey office building of moderate height is unique in many ways but the unusual geometry of the outside wall dominates the spirit of uniqueness. At the outset, let us examine the geometry: a series of undulating walls.

There is a host of mathematically rigorous surfaces that can be generated by straight lines: the circular cylinder; an infinite variety of non-circular cylinders; the cone in a variety of forms; hyperbolic paraboloids and the like. For this building, the architects eschewed all of these rigorous forms and set out to generate completely arbitrary curving surfaces without concern for the use of straight lines in the development of the form. The results are visually breathtaking but extremely expensive to construct. Enter, then, the engineer who can assist in building the stuff of dreams by introducing a level of discipline into the whole.

Imagine first a shape chosen in plan at the ground level – the shape being totally arbitrary, without mathematical definition – and then take a second arbitrary shape, totally different from the first, perhaps from the uppermost floor of the proposed building (again without mathematical definition). Now imagine that both shapes are redefined by higher-order polynomials so as to fit the chosen form, and to fall within a few millimetres of that arbitrary shape at all locations in the plan. Finally envision straight lines that pass from the upper level to the lower level but without these lines in any way maintaining a parallel relationship.

The result is a mathematical definition of the arbitrary shape of the building, but generated by non-parallel straight lines which allow the building facade to be constructed from elements that curve in one direction only.

In essence, the architect carves the mathematically arbitrary shape from a solid block and the engineer fits a definable shape to that same solid block. The exterior wall of Berlin Alternative is defined in this manner: the dream of the architect and that of the engineer are integrated to form a common dream. But why bother? Why is it so important that the plan surfaces be definable or that straight-line generators be used?

(8)

even the *laissez-faire* solution of leaving everything: height, density, Parzellierung to the entrepreneur. Rather, they choose to control Friedrichstadt by means of height restrictions, Parzellierung restrictions and, most importantly, by giving the Friedrichstrasse itself a room-like architectural unity, by eliminating projections, indentations and setbacks and preserving the cornice line of twenty-two metres for the entire length of the street.

Within this framework, land developers are allowed variations of design and material with emphasis on stone and traditional materials. Dr Stimmann, the present incumbent of Schinkel's original post, Baudirektor, has a clear perception of his goal: the buildings lining the street will reflect the Senate's wishes.

For me, commissioned as I am by an American entrepreneur, to design one block along this new-old street, these prescriptions and instructions are a fantastic challenge. On the one hand, I believe thoroughly in the right of a city to employ an architecture of its own in new sections of a town. On the other hand, as a Modern architect, my whole being longs for new forms, new city plans, new conformations of buildings, new relationships of building to street, of buildings to green space plus differing heights of structures and new materials for the buildings.

Dr Stimmann has settled the dilemma. Friedrichstrasse will be in essence rebuilt along basically eighteenth-century lines. Personally, I am pleased to work within these constraints; they occur in all architectural endeavours. Even Schinkel was forced to build in Gothic at the Friedrich-Werdersche-Kirche in spite of his outspoken preference for the classical. I can well believe there were quarrels even over the design of the Parthenon.

Yet, though I have the greatest respect for Dr Stimmann, I believe that other, less restrictive models are superior to the one he advocates. Therefore, to add to the confusion of voices, I have sketched a little building in a different manner, using the same site and programme as my present work on the Friedrichstrasse. I show the two sketches, one showing my design for a building that meets the current planning code and the other a building that I have been dreaming about.

(9)

The first is about as modern as a building by a Bonatz or a Behrens before the First World War over eighty years ago. Surely much has happened since then? The world has changed, has not architecture also? Even city planning? An example, the new-old city across the Rhine: Lille. The French have invited the young Dutch city planner Rem Koolhaas to masterplan a solution to the problems caused by the Channel tunnel with its new, very rapid train system. The results are not visible yet; the courage to begin anew, however, is clear.

The other design represents my very personal feeling about the state of architecture since the Deconstructivists broke the theoretical barriers to anti-geometric, anti-Euclidean, anti-Platonic design rules. The historic means that are of interest to me are clearly Finsterlin, early Mendelsohn, Bruno Taut, Poelzig and early Mies. There was something stirring in Germany in 1918-19 that still has power. Things are different now but some of the forms today are surely echoes of the Expressionist Berlin spirit. Phoenix rising from the ashes. New theories, new art. Never has architecture been so ready and so able to create.

Today city planning faces an uphill battle. The average, the ordinary, the academic, the clique-bound architects who are the jurors in competitions worldwide, the city officials afraid of public taste, subservient only too often to the money of land speculators now euphemistically renamed developers. The general taste of the public is by nature conservative, against any change whatsoever. Change requires leaders with vision.

All of the masterworks of Modernism in Berlin in the early part of the century were realised by private patrons – not by politicians. In a recent article in the *Frankfurter Allgemeine Zeitung,* Wolf Jobst Siedler names, as examples, Walter Rathenau's patronage of Behrens, the Wertheim family of Messel, the privately commissioned Faguswerk of Walter Gropius. Neither Mies' entry to the competition for the Friedrichstrasse Bahnhof of 1921, nor his entry for the Alexanderplatz of 1928 were greeted with joy. Only as a very old man was Mies commissioned to build his masterpiece, the Neue Museum. The German devotion to competitions also led to the Hansaviertel or Internationale Bauausstellung, which with rare exceptions, showed the low level of today's architecture and city planning.

Addressing the first question, the answer is obvious. Floors need to be constructed, columns need to be located and so forth. It is important that architect, engineer, contractor, space planner and others are able to define the space to be used. The high-level polynomial allows that definition without restricting the architect in the selection of form.

The second question, the use of straight-line generators for the definition of the facade, is more complex, relating more to the construction of the facade than to any other issue:

> Where the facade construction is a reinforced concrete bearing wall, the use of straight-line generators allows the construction of formwork which, for all practical purposes, is curved in but one direction. Plywood, for example, can be curved easily to such shapes. Reinforcement must be laid so that the primary steel does not curve. Where provided in moderate lengths it is a relatively simple task to curve the remaining reinforcement (which is usually lighter than primary steel) to a constant radius. Windows inserted into the concrete bearing wall can be of arbitrary shape or can be one of many geometric shapes.

> Where metal and glass facades are chosen, the mullions can follow the straight-line generators and the metal and glass panels can be faceted to fit in the space between mullions. Curving is not required. Even so, it is likely that a host of different panel shapes will ensue; all adding to the cost.

> Similarly, stone and glass facades could be constructed in the same manner. Any added cost can be held within sensible boundaries by utilising this approach.

As noted earlier, the remainder of the issues associated with the complexities of the arbitrary shape poses a few problems to the architect, engineer, contractor or space planner. Of prime importance, however, is that someone on the design team has a sensible level of computer skills; without question, the structural engineer undoubtedly needs to possess such skills.

Think of architecture alone. Berlin was once the leader: first, of course, Schinkel and his pupils led the world; second, before the First World War: Behrens, Messel, etc; and third, again immediately after that war, the great flowering of genius from Expressionism to the Modern Movement. In 1931, when Henry-Russell Hitchcock and I wrote our book, Berlin was the world centre of the movement of all architecture pilgrims. But today, forty years after the last war, unlike the Blützeit of the nineteen-twenties, Berlin has somehow never picked up.

Why not? There are as many theories as critics and commentators. Have Germans been no good since 1933? Is Modern architecture no longer of any worth? Has city planning been ineffective since classical times? Is Mies van der Rohe dead?

I refuse to believe any of these ridiculous hypotheses. Today, true enough, the problems are unique. The problems are city, not private, problems. Yet, the state and city must change, and architecture must change with it. In such a project most architects are helpless, all theoreticians impotent. The political world must change. I cannot believe that we are unable or incapable of such changes.

Surely Schinkel, Messel and Mies cannot be the end of the line for us. Surely genius lies latent in our genes. Berlin lies before the greatest decisions in its history. Take charge of it!

Ever since my speech in Berlin
3 years ago I have proceeded
along a new direction in which
I find myself now.
Since nothing comes from nothing,
I ask myself whence this new
direction. First, of course, from architects
I admire, in this case Eisenman & Gehry
Further back, from the German Expressionists;
further still, Malevitch and Rodchenko
the Soviet Constructivists. A touch of Gaudi
Le Corbusier (Ronchamp), Mies van der Rohe
(the Office Building at Bahnhof Friedrichstrasse)
Hurray for History. Hurray for CHANGE

The Lewis Guest House III

Comes obviously from the Expressionist Hermann Finsterlin, who made a similar form in 1924, about.

I love the mammalian curves, the voluptuous shapes. The organic outlines of each protuberance.

Someday it will get built. Somewhere I would build it maybe in a Reise!!

LEWIS GUEST HOUSE

LYNDHURST, OHIO

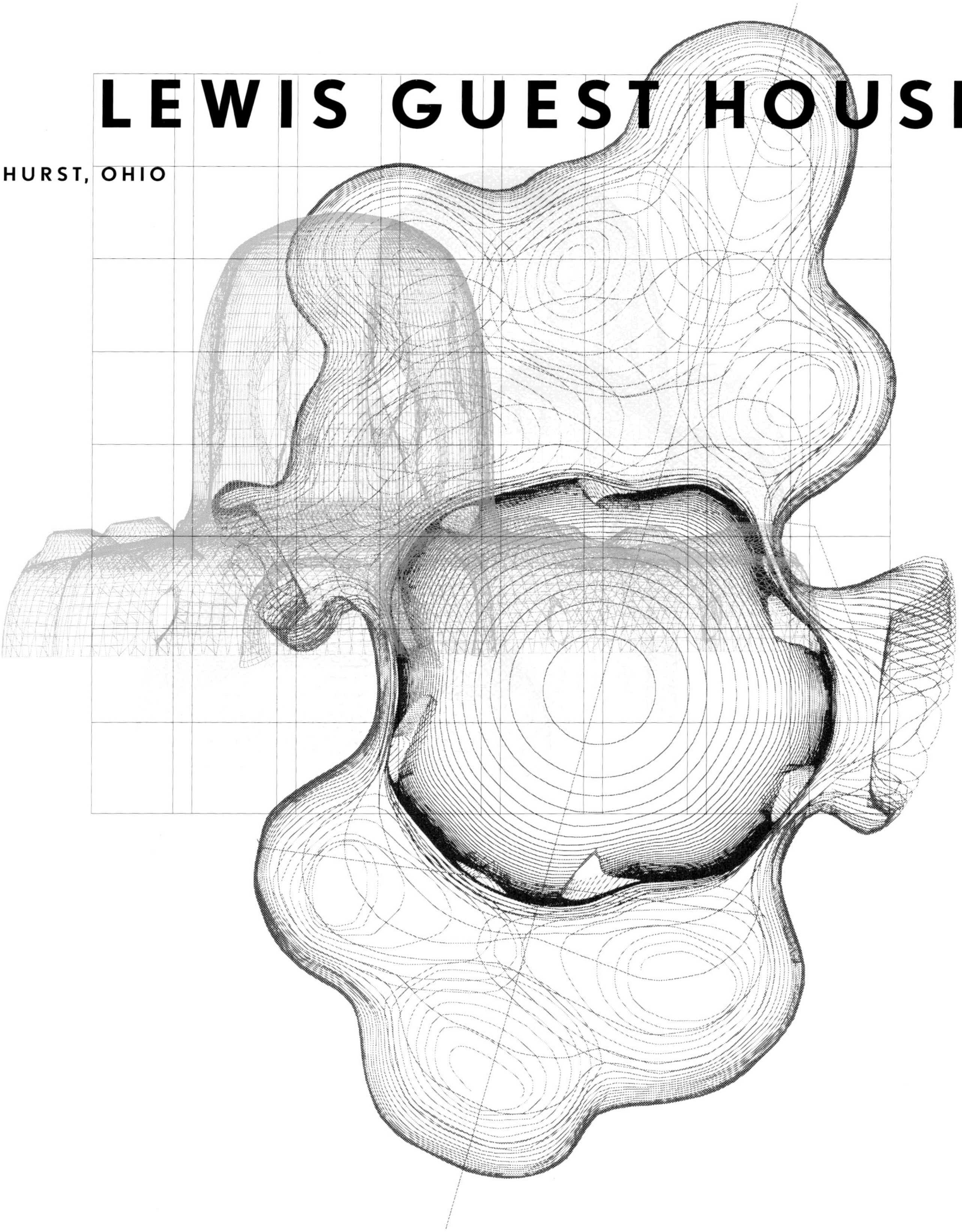

PROJECT	Lewis Guest House
DESIGNER	Philip Johnson
PARTNER	David Fiore
ARCHITECT	John Manley

1995

A GUEST HOUSE developed for a patron of the arts who wished to 'push the limits' of design and building technology, this project is an exercise in anti-Euclidian geometry exploring new construction techniques. It is also inspired by the visionary designs of the turn-of- the-century German Expressionist painters and designers. The form is dominated by a central volume, just over 11 metres in height, with complex continuous curved walls and vertical slit windows. Around this main room are clustered various smaller spaces for bedrooms, bathrooms, entry and services. Each of these smaller private rooms is top-lit by an individual skylight, completing their enclosed, womb-like nature. The entire building is placed at the edge of a pool, giving the main living room a dramatic view through a large window to the trees beyond. The construction technique involves prefabricated panels of structural wire mesh around an insulating polyurethane foam core. This is easily cut and bent to the required shape and then sprayed with concrete to complete its structural integrity.

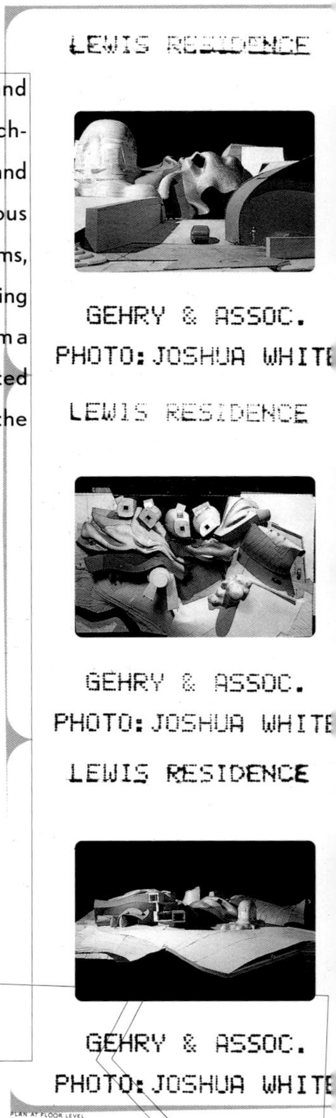

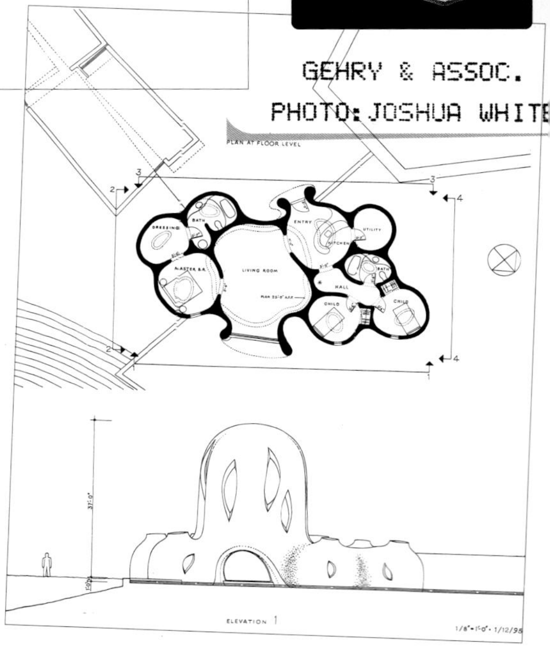

From above: The Peter Lewis Residence by Frank O Gehry & Associates; Guest House design development drawings; Opposite page, above: Plaster study model

PLAN AT 25'-0" A.F.F.
UPPER PART OF LIVING ROOM
PLAN/SECTION ABOVE
ELEVATION 1
1/8"=1'-0" · 1/5/95
ELEVATION 2
ELEVATION 3
PLAN AT FLOOR LEVEL
DRESSING
BATH
ENTRY
MASTER BR.
LIVING ROOM
CHILD
SECTION 5
1/8"=1'-0" · 1/5/95

Philip Johnson Hello Mr Gehry. **Frank Gehry** Hello Mr Johnson. **Jeffrey Kipnis** Hello Mr Gehry. **FG** Hello Mr Kipnis. **PJ** Apparently this interview will be used in the Philip Johnson Monograph, to help the book because you are such a good sell. **FG** I am? **PJ** Yes, we will put your name on the cover to guarantee sales.

INTERVIEW WITH FRANK GEHRY BY PHILIP JOHNSON AND JEFFREY KIPNIS

FG I see. **PJ** Otherwise I'll assume they would never have us work like this. **FG** Philip, you've created another monster. **PJ** Oh no! The German journalists were looking over my 'monster' so I showed them a picture of your building in *The New York Times'* Sunday article; then they said: 'well, we can see what you learned from Mr Gehry'. **FG** Yes, I know that article. **PJ** Now I want to know why you picked me, how you thought I could possibly relate to you and what it means to you to collaborate with me? **FG** Oh boy, that's a lot of questions. OK, well, the obvious reason for choosing you to do the guest house is that I love you dearly. However, I'd designed a guest house for one of your houses in Minneapolis, although you hadn't chosen me to do it, and I'm sure you freaked when you heard about it. So now I thought this new project was a chance for you to get even with me. There was also a political reason. Peter Lewis had a thing about you: he would always talk about you and your family because you're from Cleveland. I think he tried many times to hire you but each time you were busy. Maybe you sensed up front that none of this was going to go anywhere. He used to talk about his house as a collaboration with many different people. One day I thought to ask you to design a guest house for my project. It was also his birthday, so I called you in order to give you to him as a birthday present. He just loved the idea that I'd talked you into it for him – I thought he'd died and gone to heaven! **PJ** Well, I hope some of these letters I'm sending him will make him see the light. **FG** As for what I expected from the collaboration? I had no idea what to expect. We would play together in the play pen as I had done with Claes Oldenburg and David Childs, and it worked. As long as all the egos were kept intact there were no problems. First of all, I discovered that none of this could have happened without working with someone who loves architecture as much as you do. Over the years I realised this comes first; you play games, but

From above: Model view of exterior stone walls, Disney Hall, Los Angeles; section of Johnson addition to the Lewis Residence – the 'pear'; Gehry addition to the Minnesota house (1952) by Philip Johnson

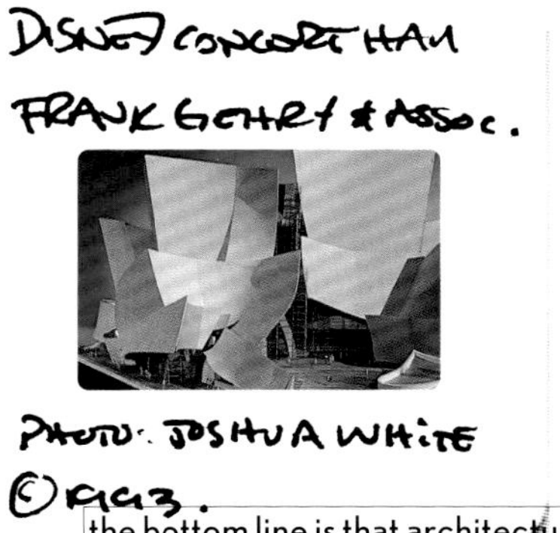

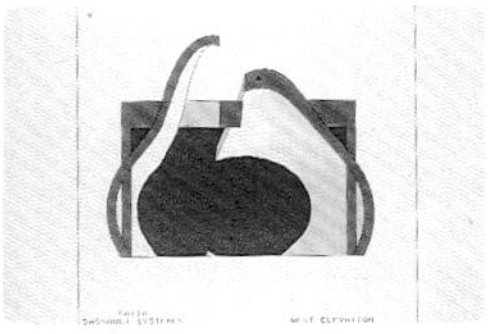

the bottom line is that architecture is the most important thing to you. **PJ** Frank, that's a lovely speech but you shouldn't just throw compliments around. **FG** No, if I'm not allowed to give compliments I'll get mad. **PJ** The main reason for the great success of the collaboration was that you left me alone, let me play in the sand. **JK** You saw three schemes: the cone and cube, the pear, and the Octopus: three radically different schemes for the same project, each of which was in some way related to what you were doing. Can you tell me your personal reaction to these three schemes? **FG** When I saw the first scheme, I was disappointed because I thought that Philip hadn't really pushed himself, and then when it was put in the context of the building, I realised that there was more method to his madness. He really had a sense of what I was doing and could play with it, putting himself in the centre of the project, without taking it over, yet maintaining an identity so that I was ultimately very comfortable with the cone and the cube. But I didn't see a lot of growth in his personal vocabulary. When we started to involve the curves, I decided that they should not be double but single curves and that there should always be an arris, albeit a curved one. So we started doing schemes with the curves. Philip started when he brought his pear into the office and I watched him play with the computer. Although I had used double curves on Disney Hall, I hadn't made an object out of them and I thought, 'Oh my God, he's pointed to a new direction', then I let that concept simmer for a while. But I learned something watching him play with the computer. I'd been resisting the computer. I hate it and the images of it. If Jasper Johns had created the visual language then maybe I would like it, but it's so awful. However, Philip waded into it as if he'd been doing it all his life. It was impressive and I was given the courage to go and try to make some sense out of it. **PJ** So, if I could give you courage Frank . . . **FG** This is true. I know you don't like to hear this and you don't agree with what I am saying, but it's not for you to say. I'm telling you my story. **JK** So, what about the last scheme? **FG** I started to toy with the double curve. I don't think Philip saw this; he was far away. However, there was discussion. Just when I was going to make the move, he made the Octopus. He did it. He pre-empted it. It was like a chess game to me. Philip was playing with the trajectory of where we were going – it was all very subtle. But then, he did it at that moment, and I freaked when the Octopus came because, damn it, he'd got there first. I loved it.

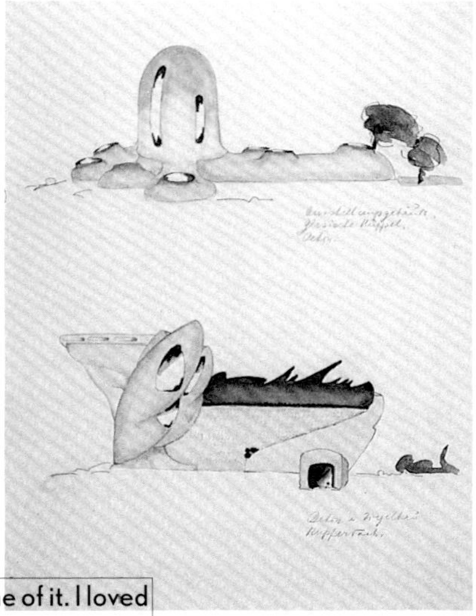

JK Is that true – you really loved it? **FG** Absolutely true, everyone knows that. I loved the game of it. I loved the fact that this super-brilliant human being could play this incredible visual chess game. **JK** Let me go into this a little more. **FG** I think this was a high-risk chess game that no one else seemed to be playing. I think that Philip, Stella and I, maybe by osmosis through the airwaves, were playing this game. **JK** At the point when Peter Eisenman saw it, my reaction was that it was so representational, it looked so much like an octopus that it actually destroyed the abstraction and even though he referred to Finsterlin, it didn't work that way; it was too close to being figurative. You didn't have that reaction? **FG** Absolutely not. **JK** And in the context of your house, which so carefully abstracts organic figures that you no longer see them as representational, I think the last guest house would have pushed your own design back towards the figurative towards the representational, and actually undermined the vulnerable abstraction of the organic in your design. You didn't see that? **FG** I didn't see that. But if you look at Philip's monster, you'll see that he wasn't going to copy Finsterlin, but make his own piece out of it instead. **PJ** Frank, I have to contradict you. After the Octopus, I went back to you and found that the most important aspect of this double curve business was the arris that you pointed out yourself. This was just mush, to quote Eisenman and he's right, though I don't agree with Kipnis: it's not organic anyway, but a little too much Finsterlin. It's just a blob. I think your arrises are what gives it the guts and the kick. Did you notice that in my later work the arrises reappear? But as far as working with you, I learned a lot more from you in those days than you ever did from me. **FG** That's not true. **PJ** Well as the German journalist said: 'Oh now we see what you learned from Gehry.' **FG** Maybe I'm terribly romantic about this because I want the world to be this way, but I'm convinced we had a visual chess game going over the airwaves. You know that feeling in the pit of your stomach when you've been pre-empted? That's the feeling, 'holy shit, he's done it! Now I have to go some where else.' So I had to make the next move and I did the little horse. But without the pear as role model, the horse's head would never have been done. **JK** Have you seen the new house in New Canaan? **FG** No, I haven't seen it, only the pictures of it. **JK** So, what do you think about it? **FG** I think it's probably fantastic, but I haven't seen the window and I heard he's had problems with the window. **PJ** How right you are Frank; to put holes in those

Above: Watercolour fantasy sketch by Herman Finsterlin, c1930; Below: Model and perspective drawing for proposed museum building in Dresden, Germany, by Frank Stella

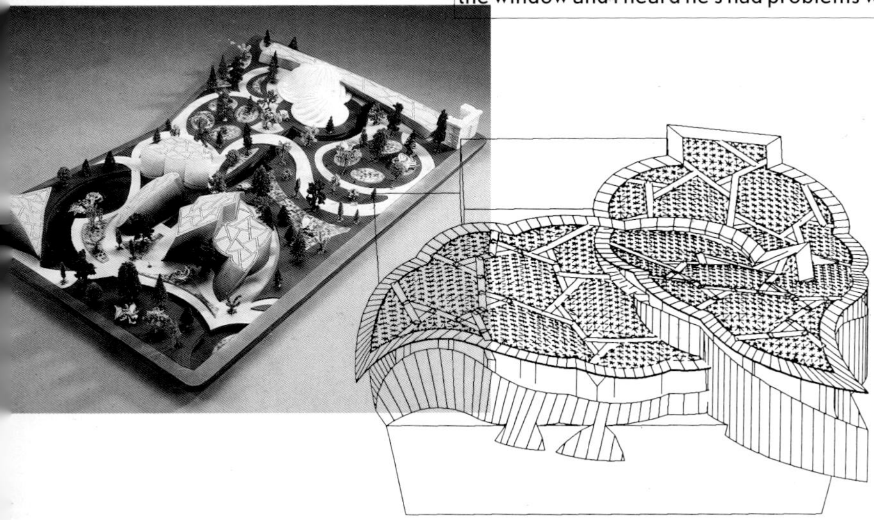

things is very hard. **FG** Yes, when Oldenburg did the binoculars I told him he had to introduce windows. And Claes said, 'Windows? So that's the difference between art and architecture – when you make a sculpture you don't have to put "windows" in it'. **PJ** But when you went to the horse's head, you didn't have the arrises? **FG** No, but there are a couple of arrises where it meets the other thing. I have since explored taking the arrises out of the horse's head, but it's not as strong. **PJ** You're like me in the guest house, which wasn't as good until I reintroduced the arrises by working with Stella. But I felt we'd hit something and that's why Kipnis is here for this exhibition at the Guggenheim. **JK** I have to say I disagree with the arrises completely. **FG** Oh God. **JK** It's a classical way of handling the topology of those intersecting surfaces and it's the place in the work when its historical antecedents are most conspicuous – in the German Expressionist work and other work like that of Steiner. **FG** The Goetheanum has arrises. **JK** Exactly, and the point is ... **FG** We're working in hard materials and eventually you have to get a window or door in there. **PJ** And you have to put windows in the soft one too, the Octopus. **FG** That was never completely solved. **JK** But the arris exaggerates the materiality – the thickness of the material, and the presence of the material – therefore undermining the formal abstraction. I think they work against each other. **PJ** I don't agree, I think you have to have it to make architecture. In fact, I was noticing the other day, there are always arrises in Art Nouveau works. **JK** Always, that's why I was saying it's a classical way of handling that topological problem. **FG** After the Lewis house for Bielefeld, we took the Octopus and started with two shapes that did not have the strength to stand next to the Serra and Johnson building. By accident we had the Octopus model at the same scale. As we were just sitting there, I picked up the Octopus and put it down in place. Eureka! It was perfect. Its central space was smaller than that of Philip's building, but it was a little taller and had the power to stand alongside it. Then the ancillary spaces, although lower and more continuous, were incorporated. This made the entrances work. I then took the form and abstracted it, making the central area a box, which quoted the Johnson building, and then added the curves to the smaller appendages and a skylight at the top. But we had only a few weeks to play with and we didn't have time for refinement, although the concept definitely came from the image of the Octopus and the

From left to right: The Goetheanum by Rudolf Steiner, c1924; model of the proposed Frank Gehry addition to the Bielefeld Art Gallery by Philip Johnson (1968); model of Peter Lewis Residence exposing the 'horse's head'

Model of Peter Lewis Residence, Frank O Gehry & Associates

organisation of it. **PJ** Frank, this is an awful lot to take into consideration. We've covered all three approaches, which is wonderful. **FG** You don't believe anything I've said to you? **PJ** Yes I do... **FG** I'd love to understand it. **PJ** I don't think that is given to us. **FG** OK. Kipnis, the arrises are important. Fuck you. **JK** OK. If you like the arrises so much, why are you trying to use glass? **FG** Because you have to put windows in the goddamn thing. **JK** Yes, but you're using glass for more than transparency. In all the models of the Lewis house there is a desire on your part to introduce inflected forms in the glass, which is actually a desire to remove the arris, as far as I can see. **FG** Yes, but I didn't win in the end. **JK** OK. The fact that you gave up and went back to the arris is one thing but... **FG** We didn't win because of all the practical considerations. We had south-facing glass, with triple glazing and to make that three-layered, wiggly glass within the realms of human cost just wasn't possible. **JK** So, the arris was the only practical compromise. **FG** But it does ground you back to life and architecture and the world we live in. **JK** It's the only classical issue left... **FG** Maybe it's always going to be there? It's certainly the strength ofthe pieces thus far. **PJ** That's perhaps the best answer. Now let's go home and get some sleep. That was a wonderful speech and I've heard everything I wanted to know.

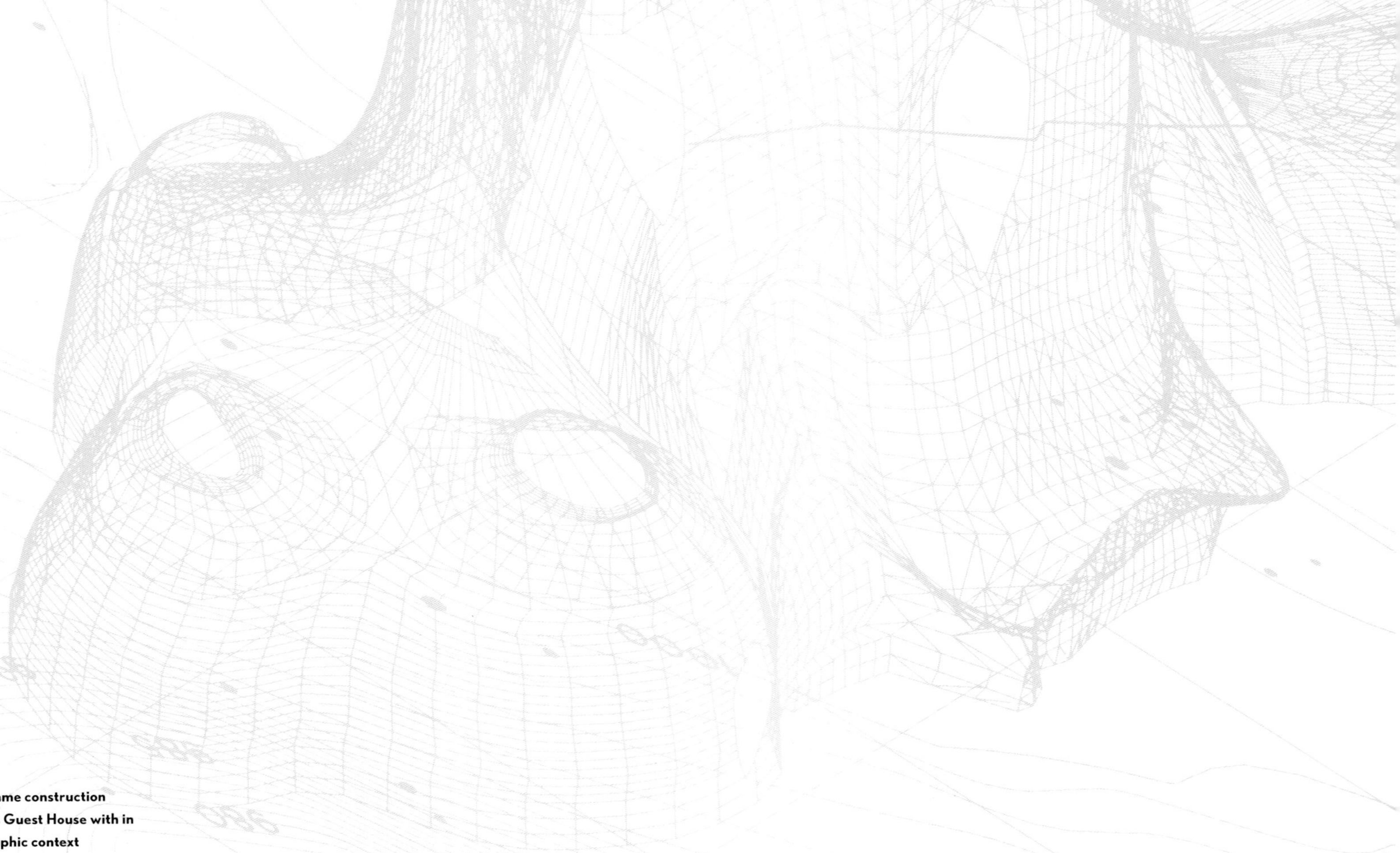

Wire frame construction of Lewis Guest House with in topographic context

NATIONAL MUSEUM

The competition model showing the main entrance and stepped entry plaza with central fountain leading to the exterior entrance court

OF KOREA

SEOUL, KOREA

PROJECT National Museum of Korea
DESIGNER Philip Johnson
PARTNER Alan Ritchie
MANAGER Christian Bjone

1995

A history museum for the Korean nation is to be located at the south end of a proposed park system and cultural complex. It has a programme for 108,000 square metres of facilities. A vast 150-metre-wide plaza with central fountain forms the start of a public procession that continues up to an enclosed outdoor courtyard with archaeological artifacts on display. The main lobby is a single room similar in dimension to the Pantheon in Rome with a 37-metre-high ceiling, which connects to the lower level education, services and parking and continues on to the general exhibition room, a central space to which all the galleries return. Each gallery is a two-storey distinct elliptical volume. The advantage of this organisation and shape is that the clear circulation looping through the galleries always returns to the central exhibition room providing the reorientation necessary in such a huge public complex.

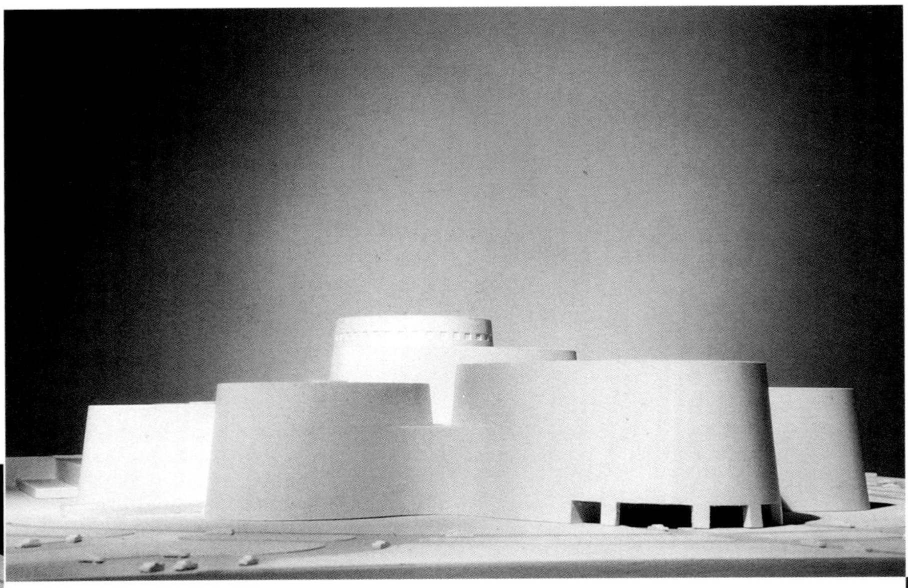

The competition model illustrates the aerial view, north bus entry and views from garden hills

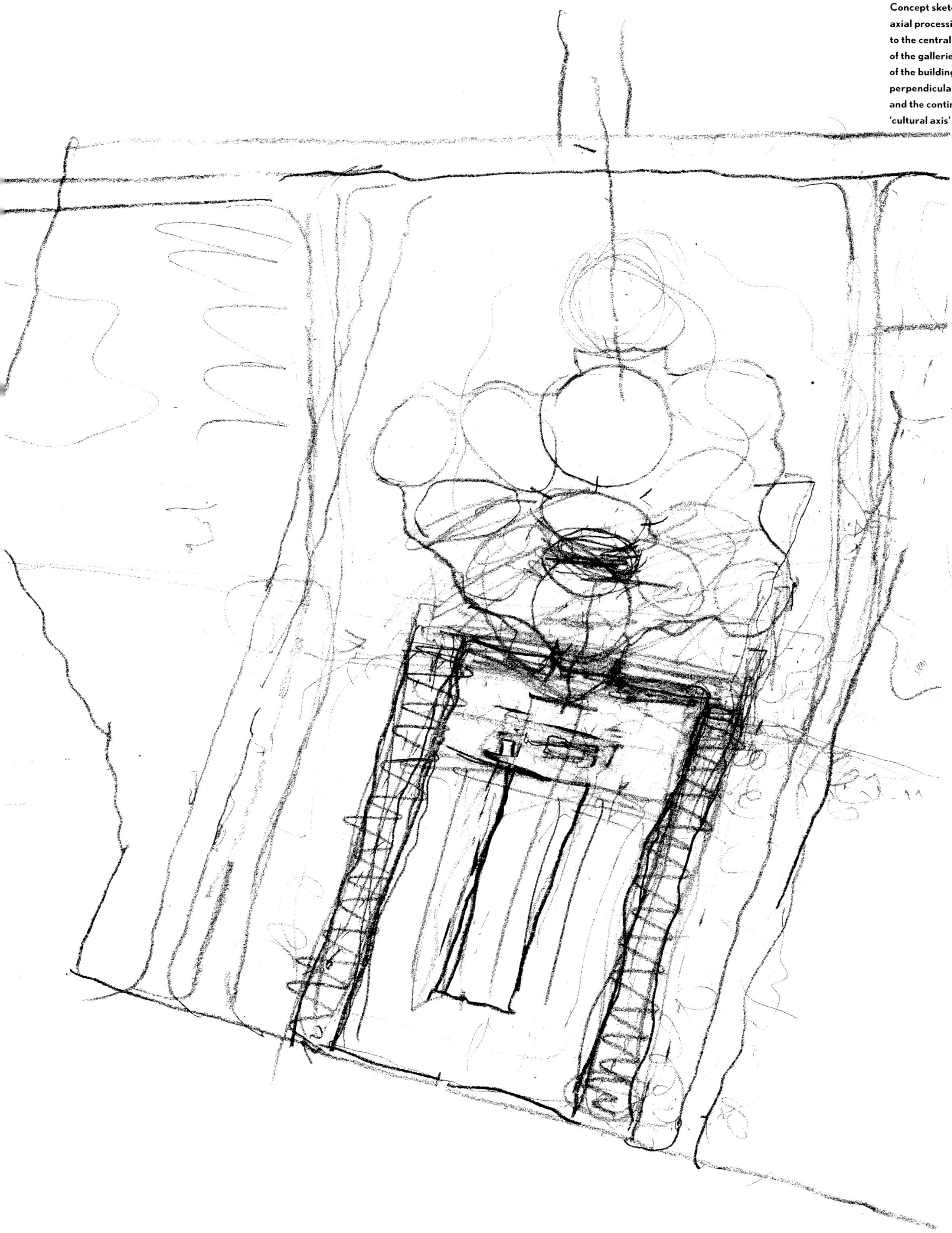

Concept sketch relating the axial procession of the plaza to the centralised organisation of the galleries. The rotation of the building allows entry perpendicular to the main street and the continuation of the 'cultural axis' from the north

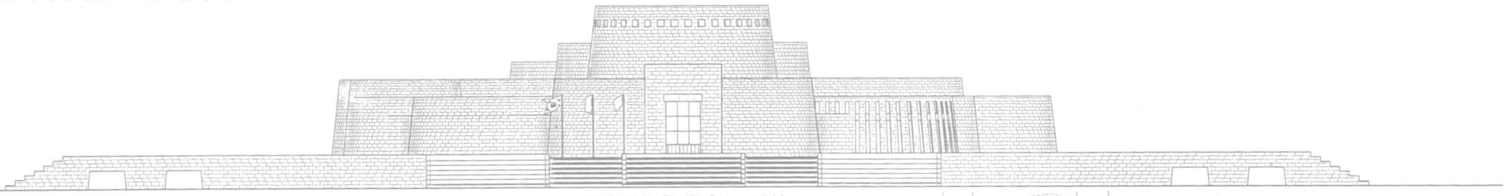

FRONT ELEVATION *1:500*

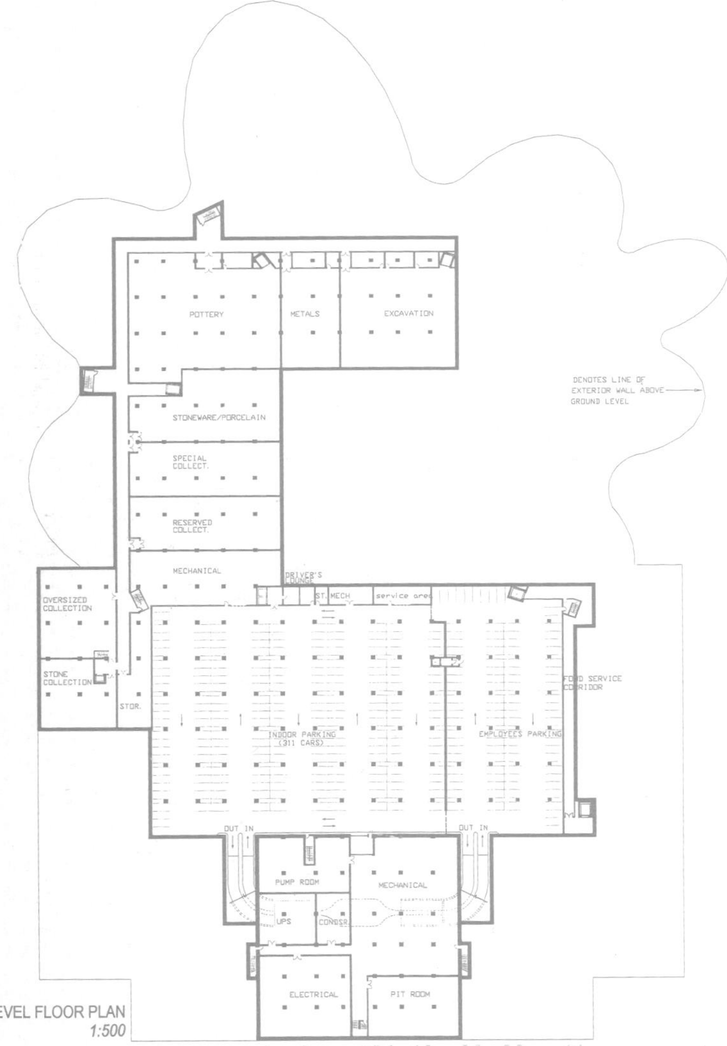

LOWER LEVEL FLOOR PLAN
EL. + 13.0 *1:500*

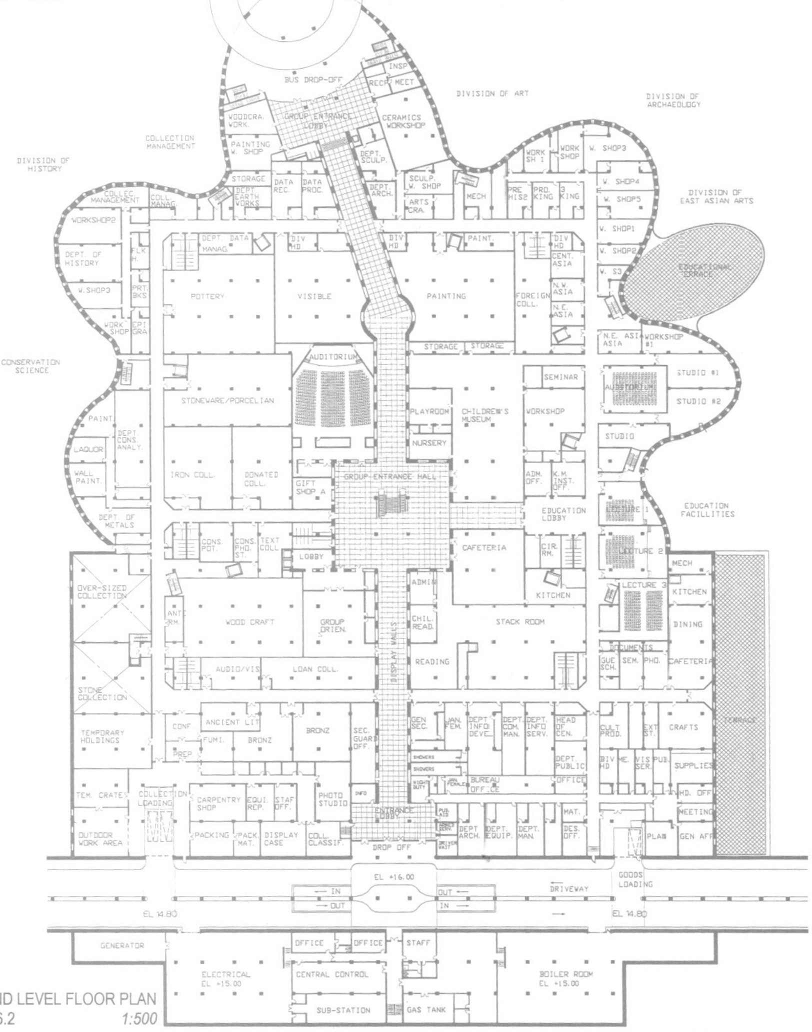

GROUND LEVEL FLOOR PLAN
EL. + 16.2 *1:500*

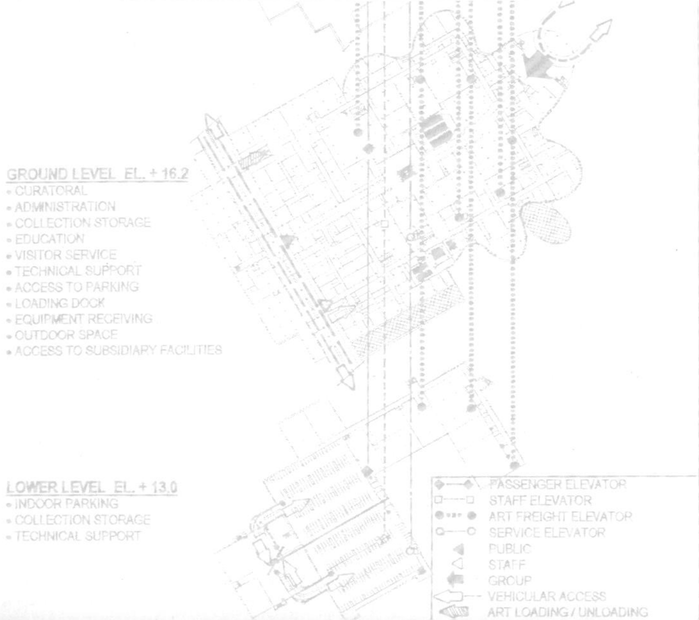

SITE SECTION (SOUTH - NORTH) *1:1200*

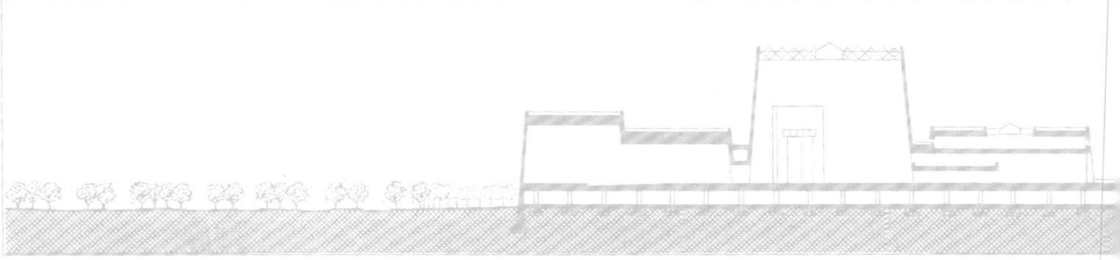

SITE SECTION (EAST - WEST) *1:1200*

ROOF LEVEL EL. + 40.0
- Roof terraces over the Members Restaurant and Donors Collection are connected by an elevator lobby serving all levels.

MEZZANINE LEVEL EL. + 33.5
- Executive Administration is connected by an elevator lobby serving all levels.

UPPER GALLERY LEVEL EL. + 30.0
- The five Permanent Exhibition Galleries are located clockwise around the Central Exhibition Hall.
- The Temporary Exhibition Gallery is directly accessible from the Main Lobby.
- The Gift Shop B can be accessed from the visitor balcony of the Central Exhibition Hall.
- The Members Restaurant is accessed from the Main Lobby and Entrance Court.
- Multiple air handling systems, adjacent to each gallery, provide for special environmental needs.

MAIN GALLERY LEVEL EL. + 22.5
- The five Permanent Exhibition Galleries are located clockwise around the Central
- Central Exhibition Hall acts as the primary link to the immediately surrounding exhi
- The Temporary Exhibition Gallery is directly accessible from the Main Lobby.
- Coatrooms, ticket counters, an information kiosk and the main Gift Shop are locate Lobby.
- The Restaurant can be accessed from the Main Lobby and Entrance Court.
- The 900 - seat Theater is directly off the Main Lobby .
- Multiple air handling systems, adjacent to each gallery, provide for special environ
- The Entrance Court is the gathering place for visitors prior to entering the Main Lob
- Bridges connect the Grand Plaza with the Museum Park Outdoor Parking.

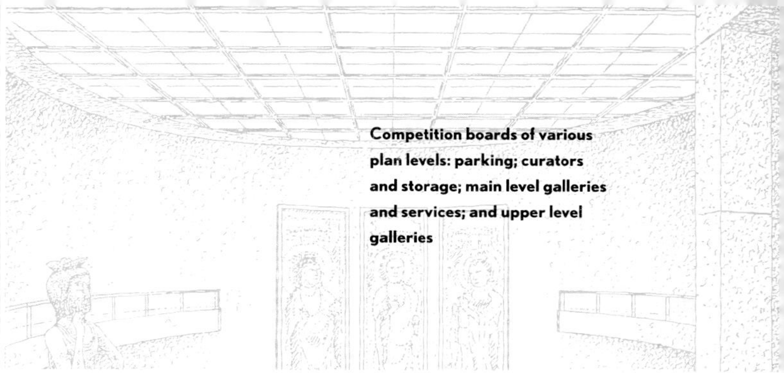

Competition boards of various plan levels: parking; curators and storage; main level galleries and services; and upper level galleries

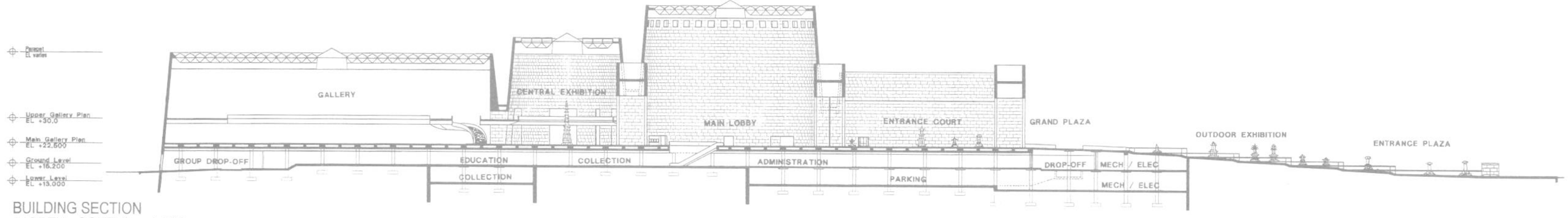

BUILDING SECTION
(NORTH - SOUTH) *1:500*

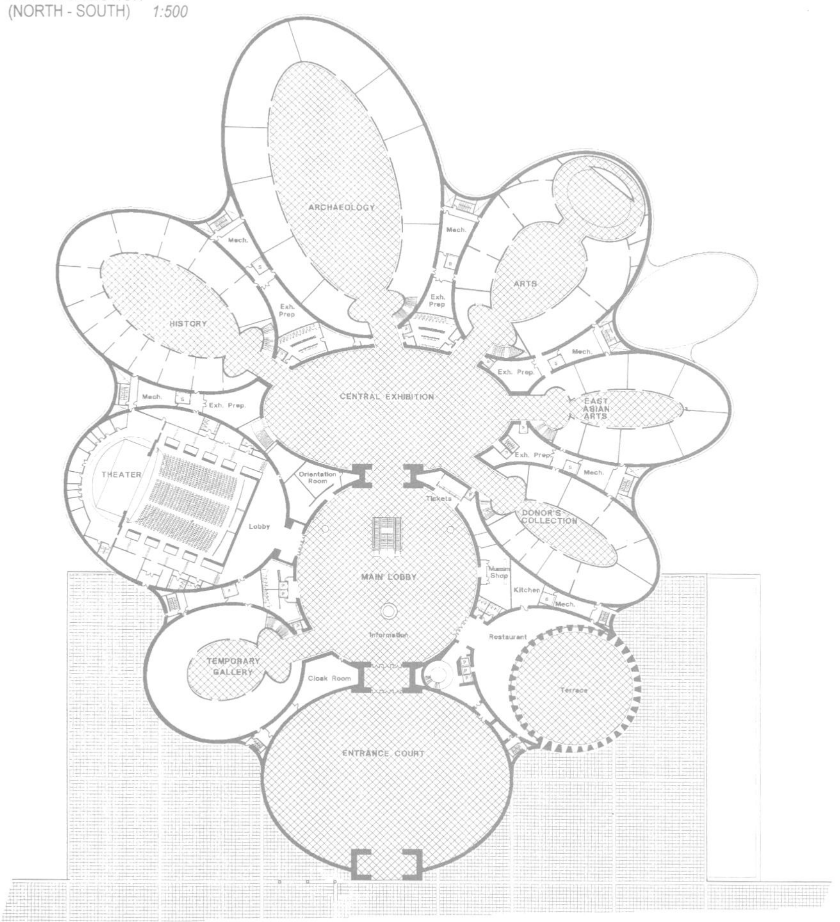

MAIN GALLERY LEVEL FLOOR PLAN
EL. + 22.5 *1:500*

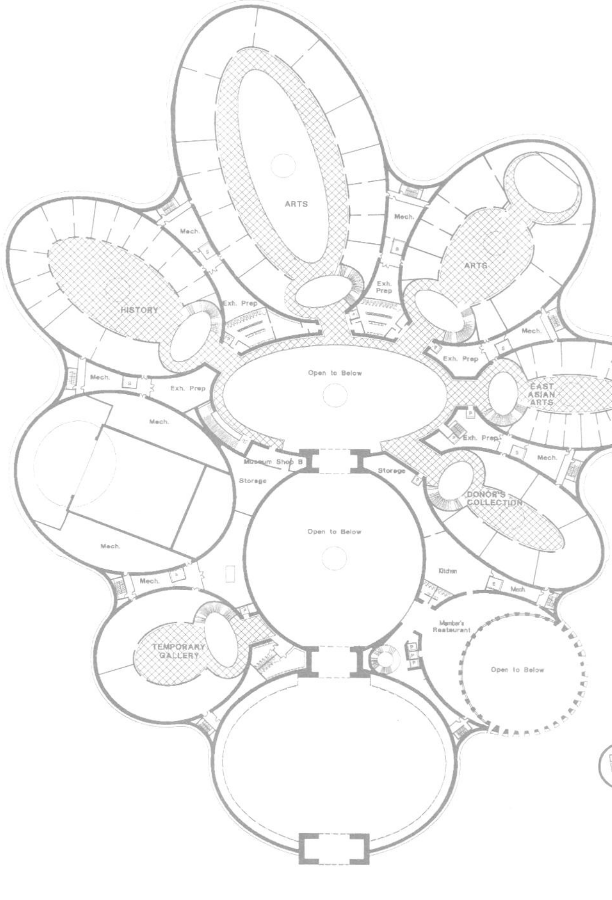

UPPER GALLERY LEVEL FLOOR PLAN
EL. + 30.0 *1:500*

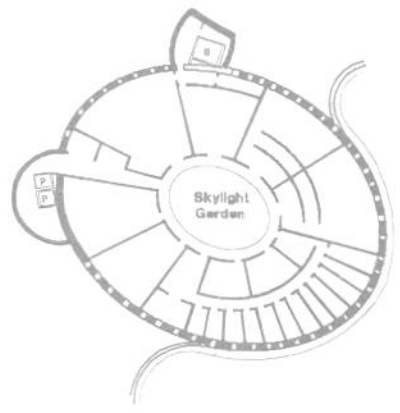

MEZZANINE LEVEL
(ADMINISTRATION) *1:500*

PROJECT
National Museum of Korea

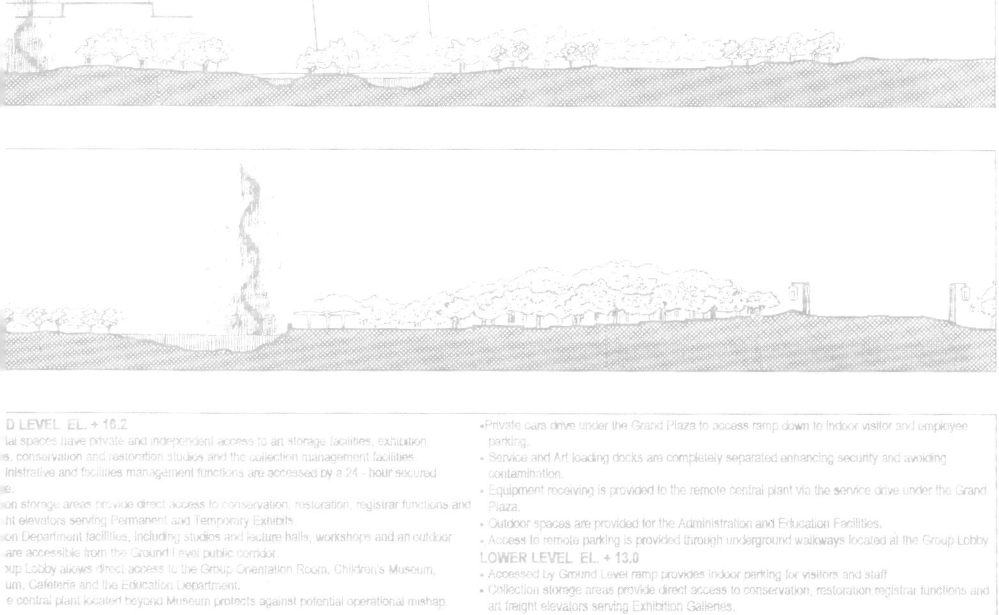

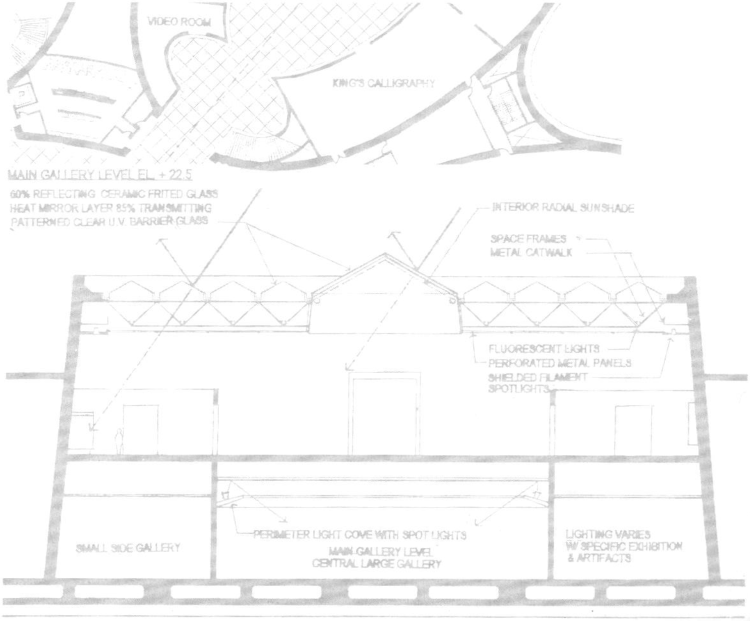

The National Museum of Korea

Philip Johnson

Ease of orientation was the prime concern in the design of the National Museum of Korea: the effortless transition from storage to exhibit room; ready assessment of the visit ahead; ease of access to ancillary requirements - toilets, restaurants, shops, theatres, auditoriums - not to mention access from both the north and the south, outside the control points.

Perhaps no museum of such a size has ever been built in one programmatic effort. The great museums of New York and Paris, for example, have been built over the centuries and are still hopelessly inadequate for visitor access. In the design process, such requirements were kept in mind. So too was the aim of creating a building massing that would be more pleasing than overwhelming, more Korean than international and more 'user-friendly' to a vast public.

There are two main levels: the ground level and the first floor level. The ceremonial south entrance is on the upper level. The bus entrance is to the north, on the ground level. These entrances lead out from a north-south spine that runs directly through the building, meeting at an escalator in the main entrance hall. The main entrance hall, which is very large and is the highest element of the design, some 40 metres high, is a mixing place for all of the required activities. The main route leads directly north into the central exhibit area, and is the control point for all the subsidiary exhibition galleries.

The exhibition areas are divided into four separate 'pods', each of which represents one of the required groupings as suggested in the programme. Each 'pod' is then subdivided into small galleries around the outside and a great central gallery.

The exterior of the building is a grouping of large and medium-sized elliptical ovoid structures, connected on the lower level by a meandering wall. This gives the effect on the outside of there being a group of middle-sized ovals clustered around the main entrance hall.

The catch words in the process of the design were clarity, accessibility and monumentality. The first and second are the most important, functionally and practically; the third is the most important historically, aesthetically and spiritually. Clarity is obviously the strong point. No-one wants to get lost in a building of this size. The goal of accessibility has been achieved throughout the museum. Parts of the exhibition can be closed without affecting the other exhibits; all the exhibit 'pods' are directly accessible from the storage unit below; and the theatres, shops, restaurants and toilets are readily found near to the exhibit rooms. The pathway from the front door is straight, or nearly straight, to facilitate orientation and each 'pod' is located in such a way that guided tours may proceed through an exhibit area without having to retrace their steps. Finally, all outdoor exhibitions are accessible from the main entrance hall. Monumentality has been emphasised by high ceilings, Korean granite wall surfaces and by the gentle curves of the outer walls.

Not only does the National Museum of Korea stand as a symbol of achievement and Korean individuality, it also hopes to make a contribution to world museology while also creating a lodestar for international design.

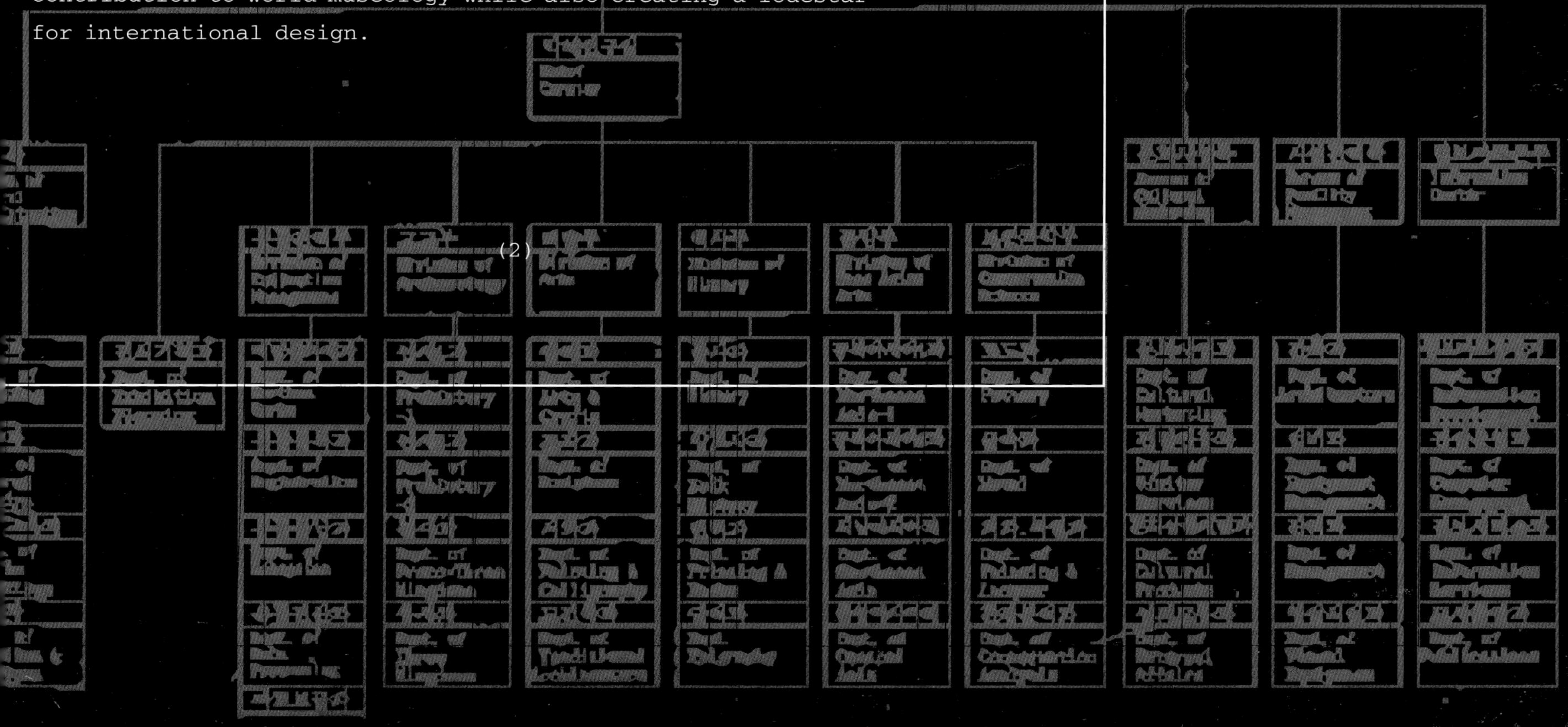

(2)

SETON HILL

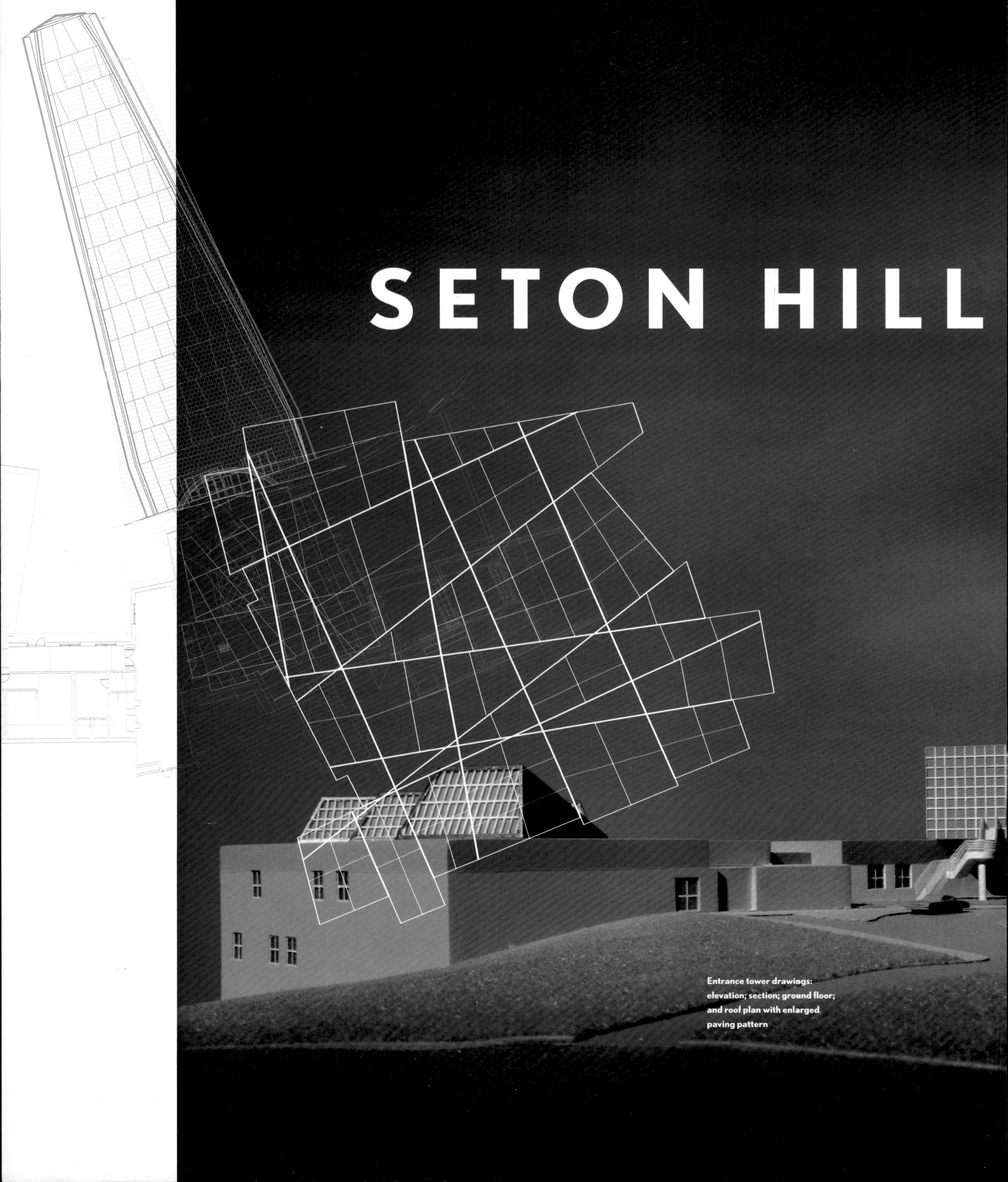

Entrance tower drawings: elevation; section; ground floor; and roof plan with enlarged paving pattern

FINE ARTS CENTER

GREENBERG, PENNSYLVANIA

PROJECT Seton Hill Fine Arts Center

DESIGNER Philip Johnson

MANAGERS David Harrison, Don Porter

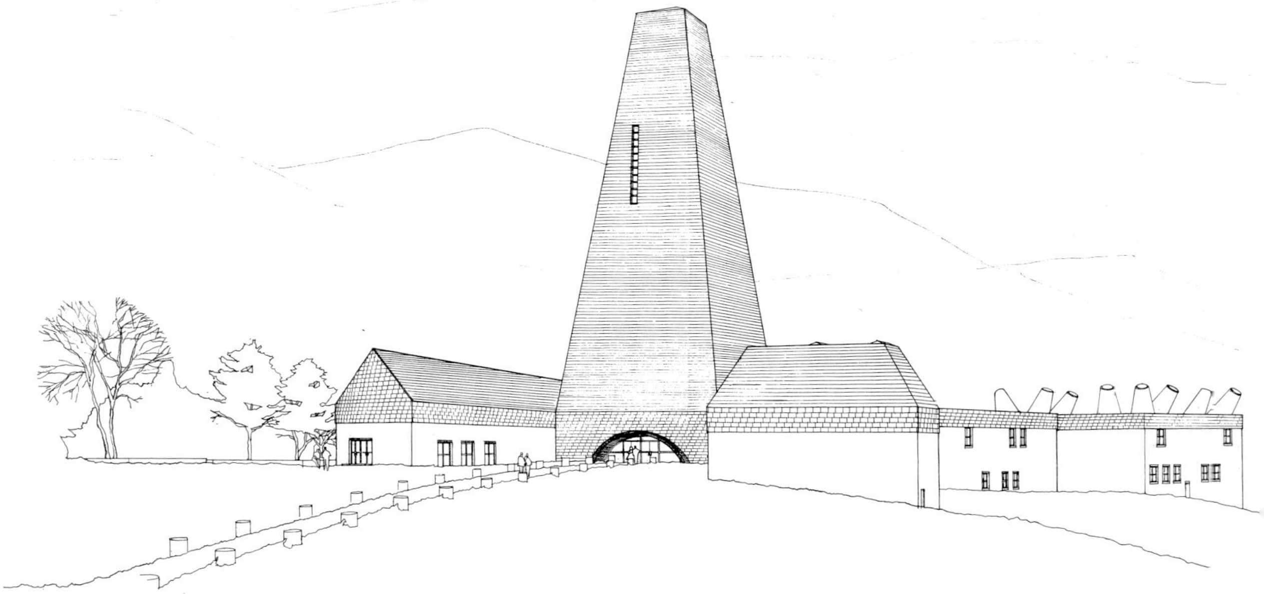

1990

The project is a new fine arts facility for a small, private liberal arts college in Greenberg, Pennsylvania. The major functions are a 600-seat theatre, a 180-seat flexible theatre, ancillary production areas, performance spaces, art studios, classrooms, offices, an art gallery and an entrance pavilion, all within 30,400 square metres of enclosed space. Located at the top of a hill, 90 metres from the nearest school building, the grouping of component structures is reminiscent of an Italian hill town with a 45-metre-tall entrance tower acting as the campanile. The facility is organised around the entrance tower, with the theatre wing off to one side, the art gallery to another and studios and classrooms in a third direction. All fasciae and sloping roofs are covered in lead-coated copper with the remainder of the skins clad in a variety of rich, double-fired glazed brick. Colours are red, black, yellow, green, grey and blue. All metalwork is white.

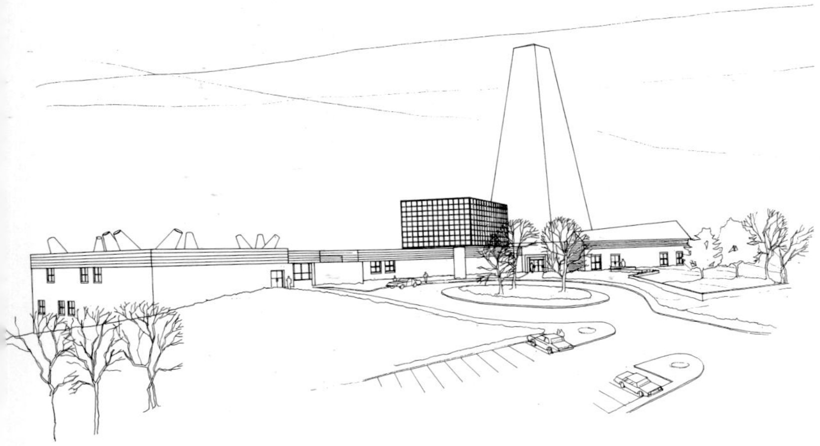

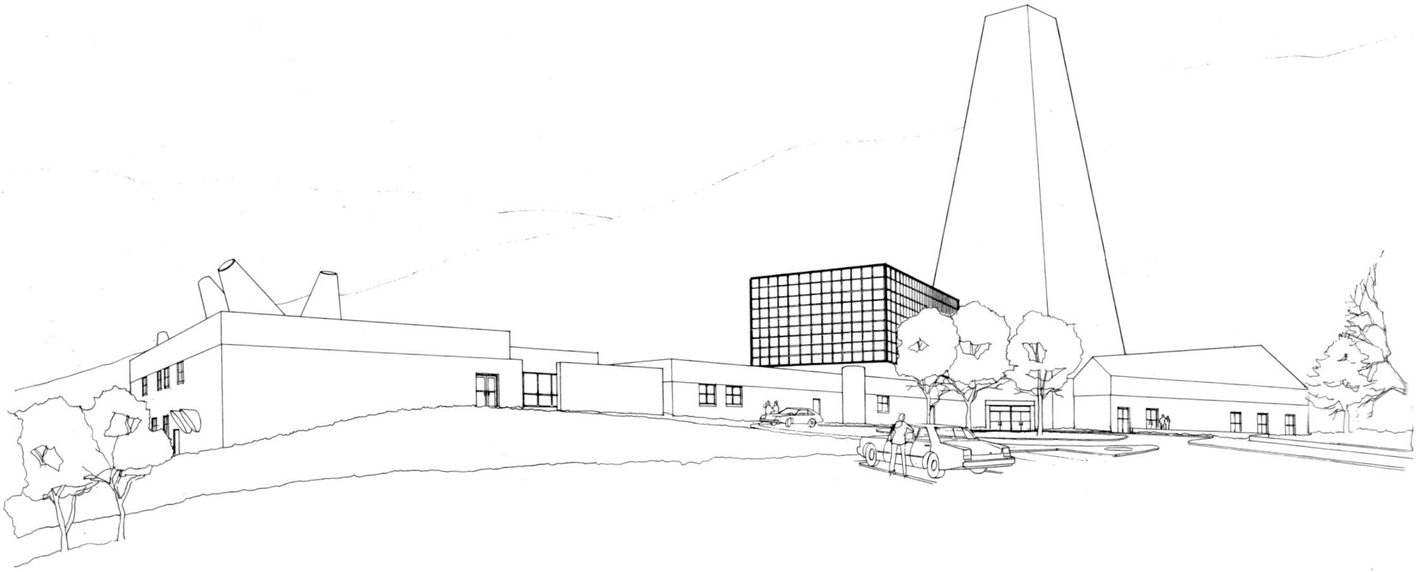

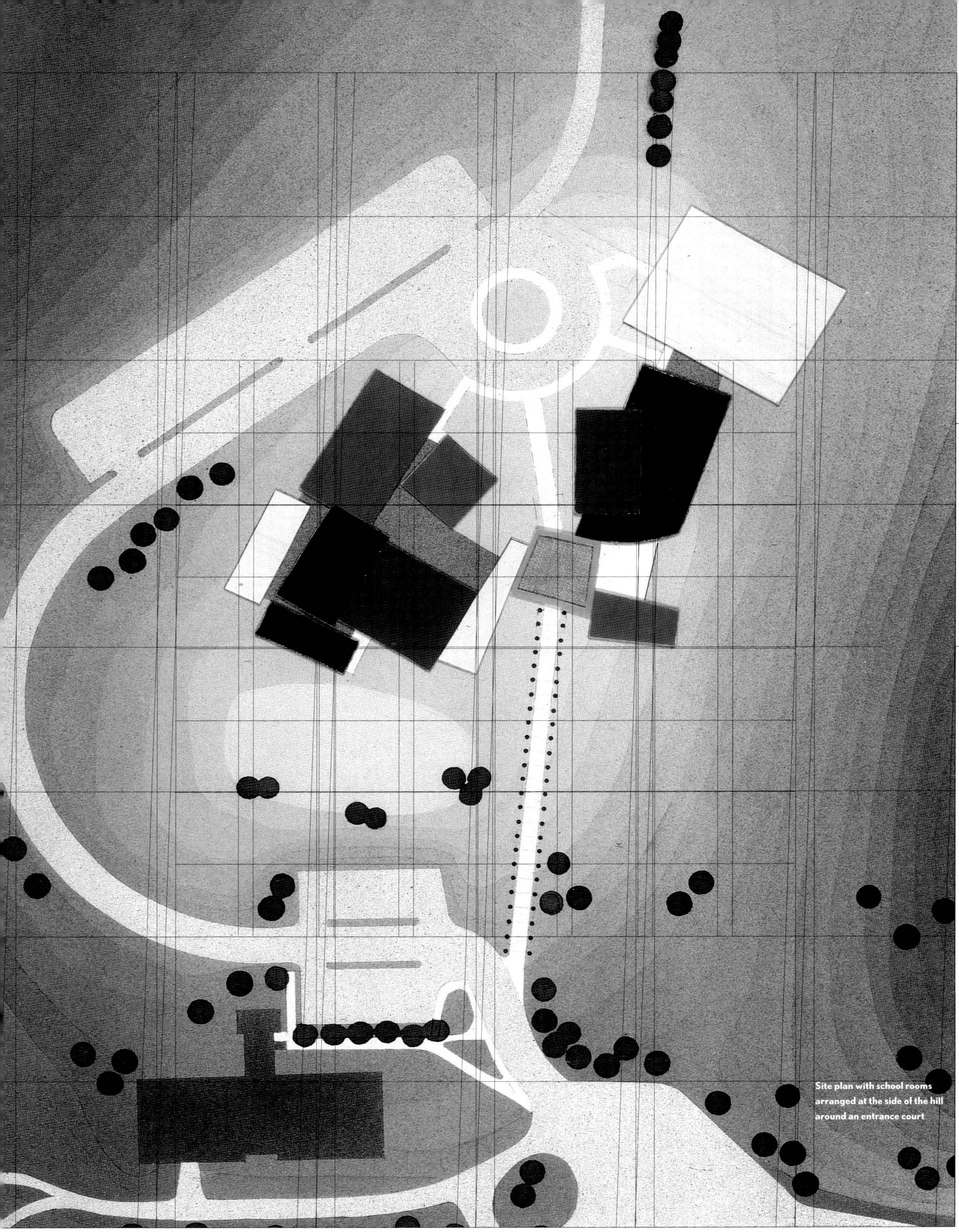

Site plan with school rooms arranged at the side of the hill around an entrance court

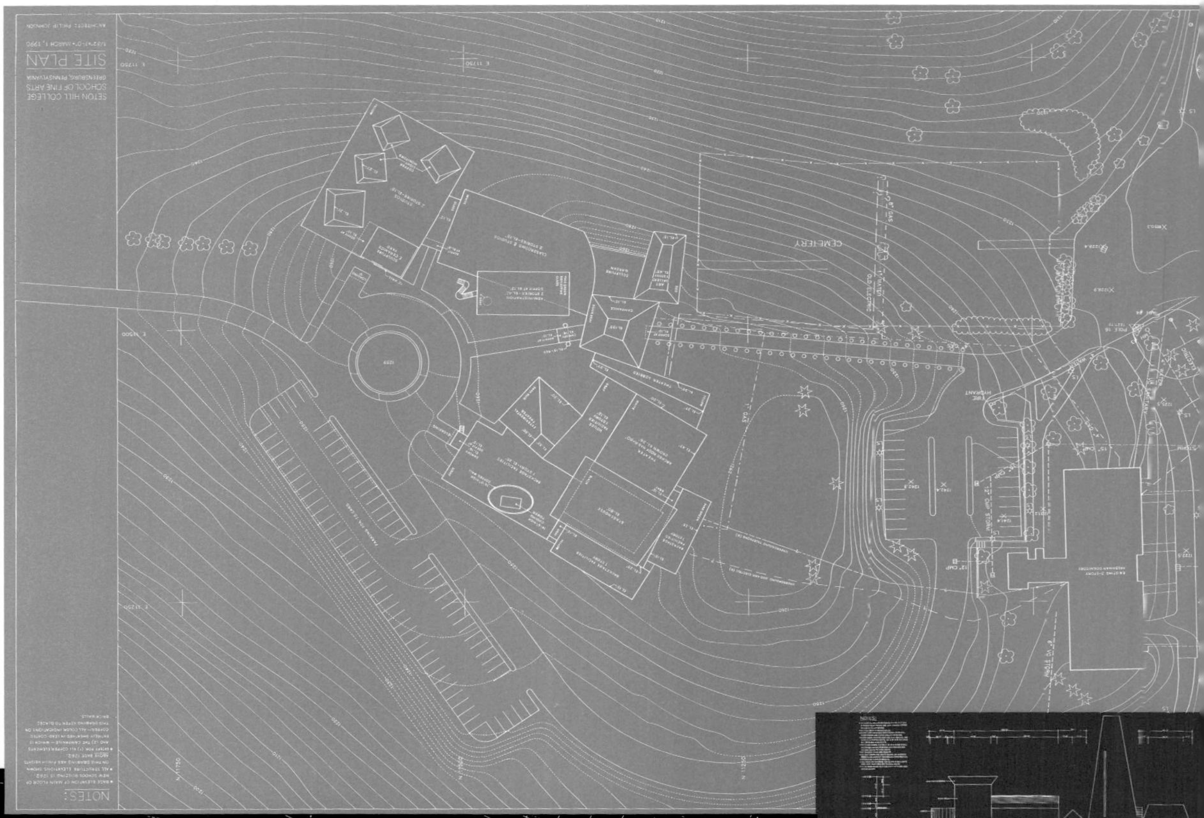

MECHANICAL ROOM No.5
COSTUME STORAGE
PROP STORAGE
TRAP ROOM
ORCHESTRA PIT
UNEXCAVATED
STORAGE
VIDEO CONTROL ROOM
VIDEO VIEWING
MECHANICAL ROOM No.1
LOBBY
METALSMITHING
WOODWORKING
STORAGE
MECHANICAL ROOM No.2
PHOTOGRAPHY
FABRICS
GRAPHICS AND CALLIGRAPHY
CEMETERY
SETON HI
SCHOOL O
GREENSBURG
BASE

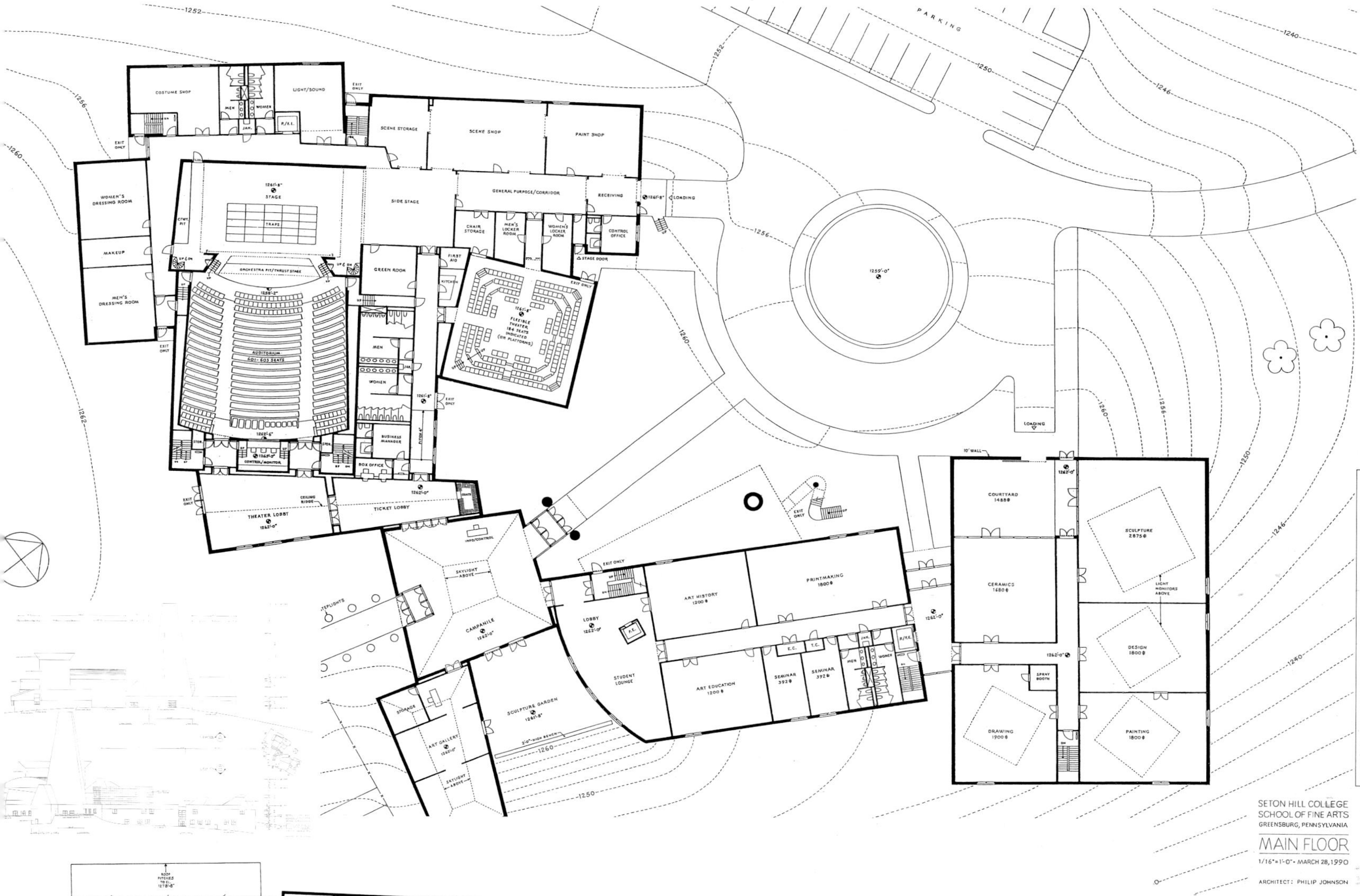

Construction drawings of site plan, basement levels, ground floor and upper level

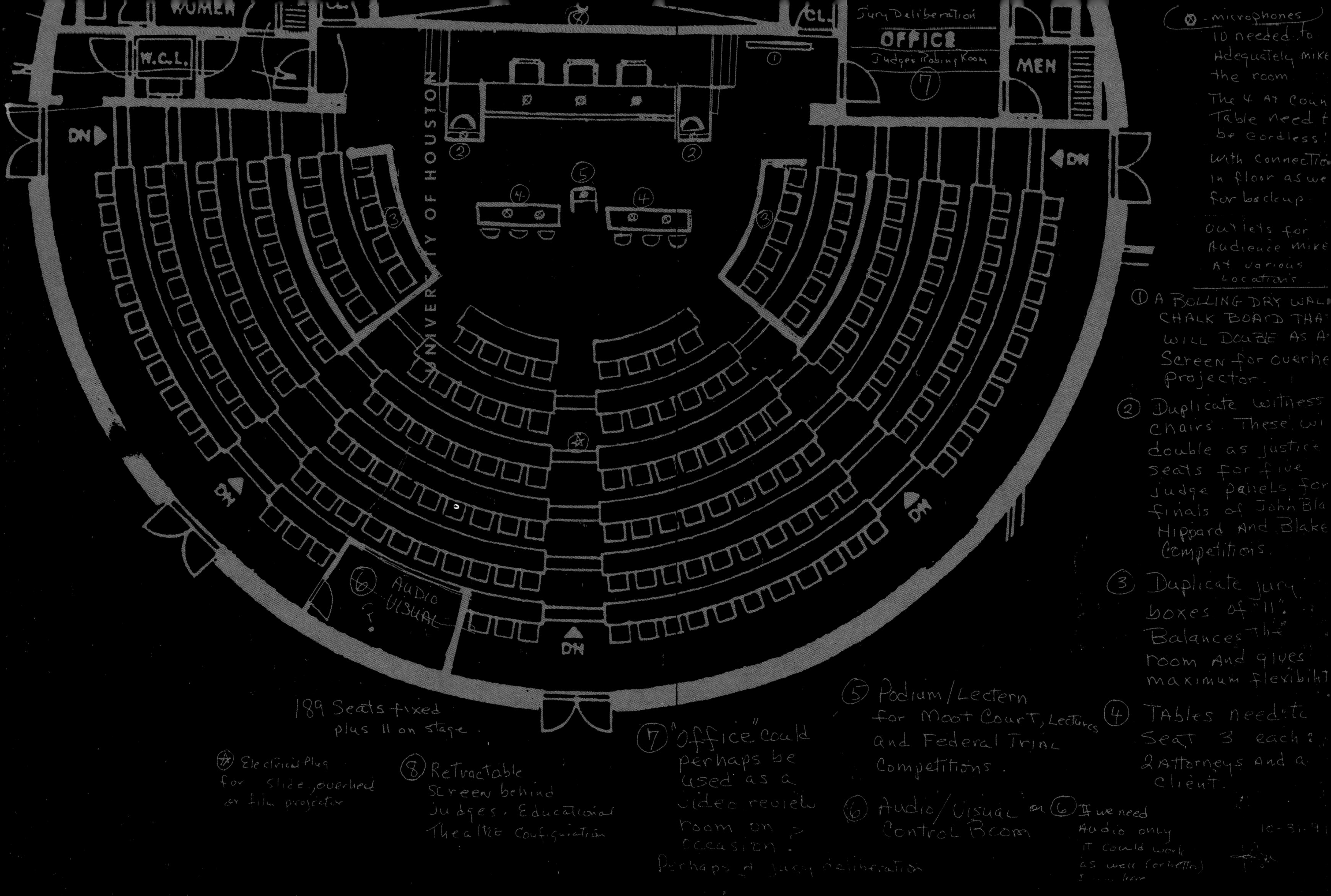
UNIVERSITY OF HOUSTON
WOMEN
W.C.L.
MEN
CL.
OFFICE
Jury Deliberation
Judges Robing Room
AUDIO VISUAL ?
DN
189 Seats fixed
plus 11 on stage.
Electrical Plug for Slide, overhead or film projector
⑧ Retractable Screen behind Judges. Educational Theatre Configuration
⑦ "Office" could perhaps be used as a video review room on occasion?
Perhaps a jury deliberation
⑤ Podium/Lectern for Moot Court, Lectures and Federal Trial Competitions.
⑥ Audio/Visual Control Room
or ⑥ If we need Audio only it could work as well
microphones
10 needed to Adequately mike the room.
The 4 at Coun Table need to be cordless!
With connections in floor as we for backup.
Outlets for Audience mikes At various Locations
① A ROLLING DRY WALL CHALK BOARD THAT WILL DOUBLE AS A Screen for overhead projector.
② Duplicate witness chairs. These will double as justice seats for five judge panels for finals of John Bla Hippard And Blake Competitions.
③ Duplicate jury boxes of "11". Balances The room And gives maximum flexibility
④ TABles need to Seat 3 each: 2 Attorneys And a client.

LAW CENTER ADDITION

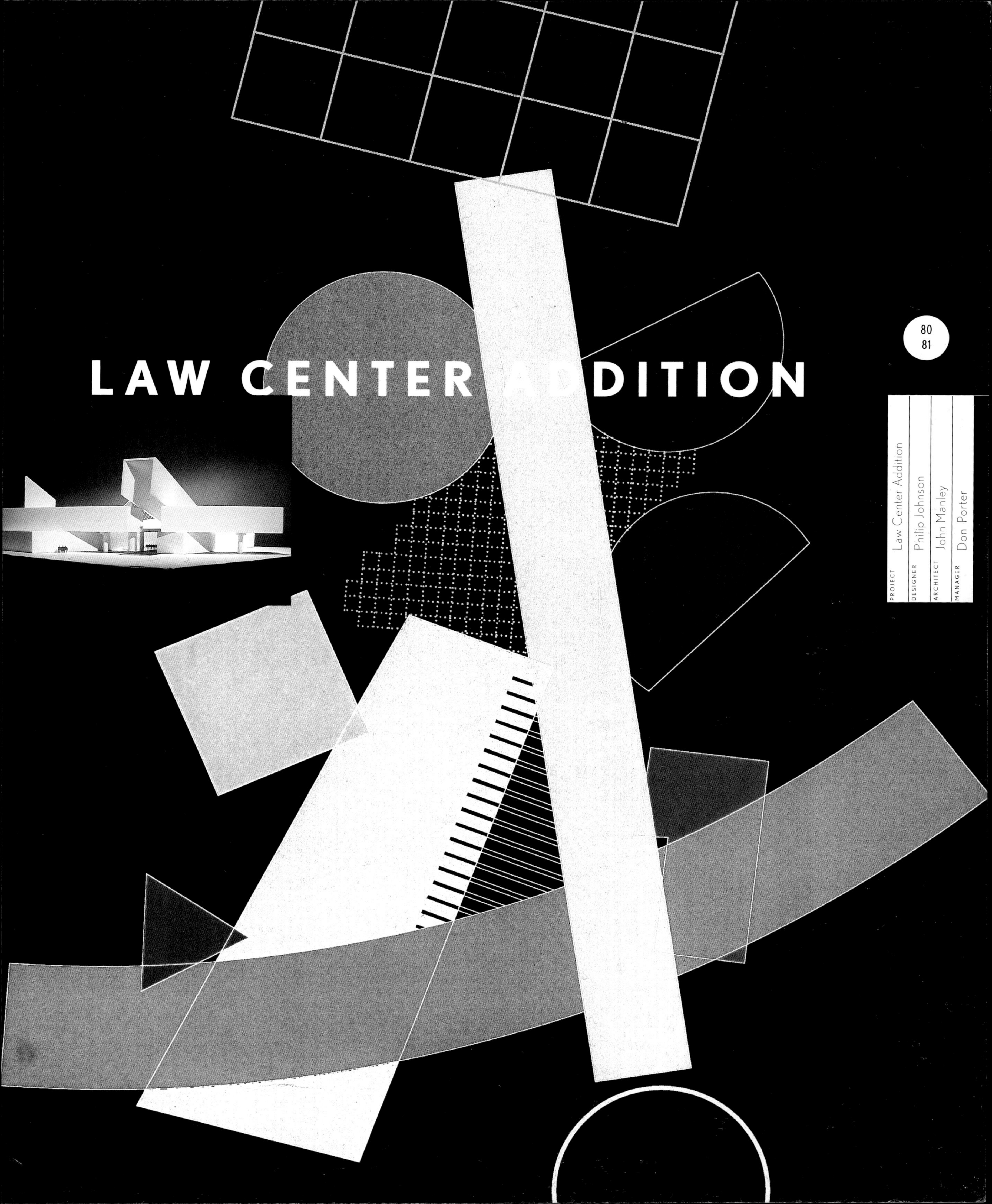

PROJECT Law Center Addition
DESIGNER Philip Johnson
ARCHITECT John Manley
MANAGER Don Porter

1991

This new 12,000-square-metre facility is conceived as a 'street of law' where the interface between faculty and students will occur in an open, covered promenade. This 'street' proceeds from the formal entrance to a tent-covered plaza at the centre of the school. Each individual function is given a different shape and colour and is attached to the street and its sloping roof. The office block is a curved, curtain-walled element raised on stilts that is split by the canopied street. The remaining courtrooms, cafeteria, seminar rooms and student centre are clad in richly coloured double-fired brick. The canopy over the street will be lead-coated copper.

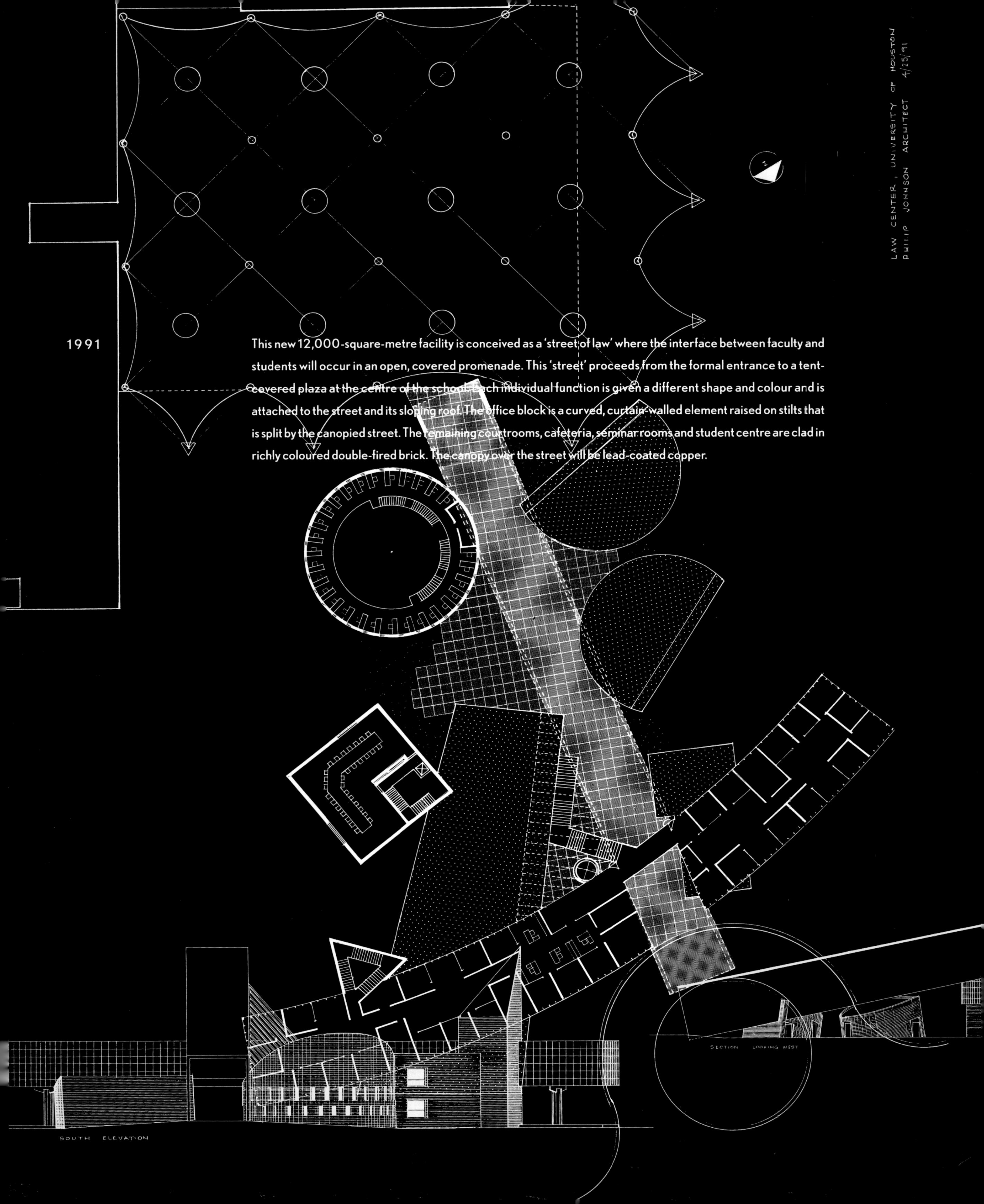

PROJECT
Law Center Addition

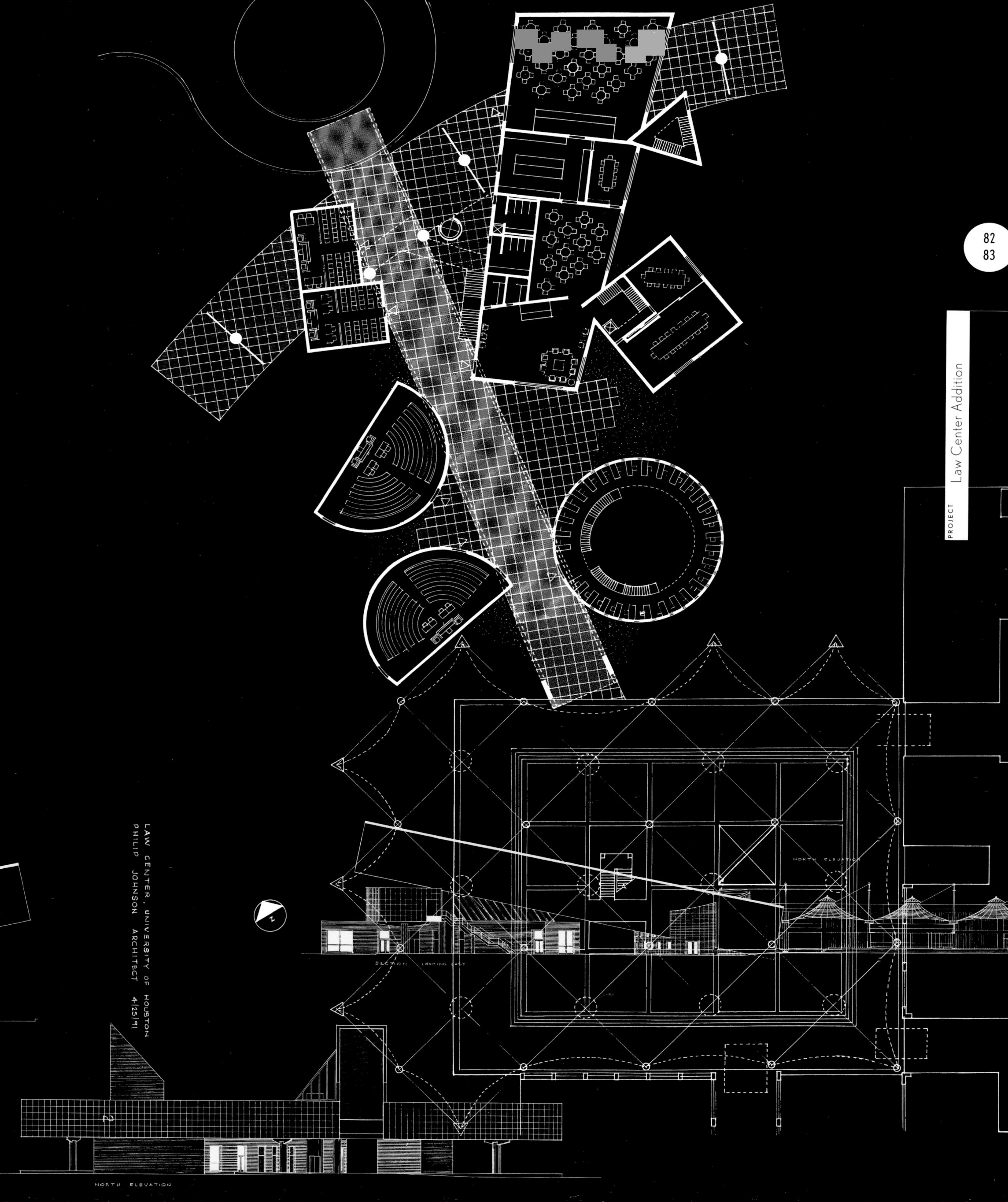

ST BASIL

UNIVERSITY OF ST THOMAS, HOUSTON, TEXAS

CHAPEL

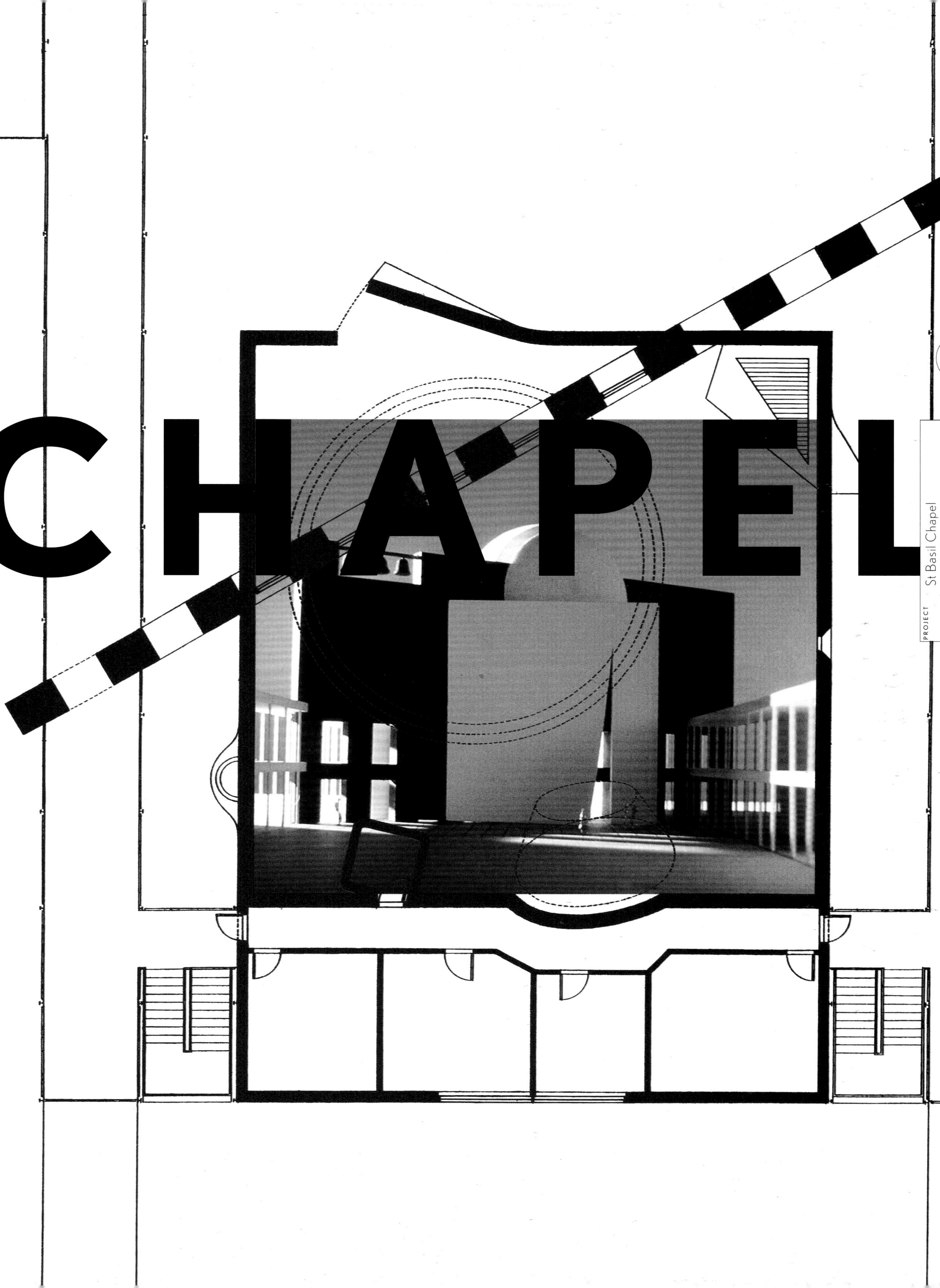

PROJECT St Basil Chapel
DESIGNER Philip Johnson
PARTNER David Fiore
ARCHITECT John Manley

1996

The chapel is a cube of 15.2 metres square surmounted by a cleft dome and seating 225. Situated on a campus designed by Philip Johnson, and built in 1957, it is surrounded on three sides by a two-storey gallery connecting the existing buildings. The cube is 'sliced' at an oblique angle by a punctured black granite stone wall which ends by 'crashing' through the galleries on both sides. It is perforated by doorways, windows and an opening for bells. The cube is white stucco, inside and out, and the entrance is a warped wall that projects outward like a tent flap. The main effect in the modest interior is the play of daylight from hidden sources: the slot through the dome above; the angled skylight above the altar; the chimney-like light over the statue of the Virgin; and the slot behind the organ. The great cross on the west wall, made of clear glass, is startling for its brightness against the comparatively dim interior.

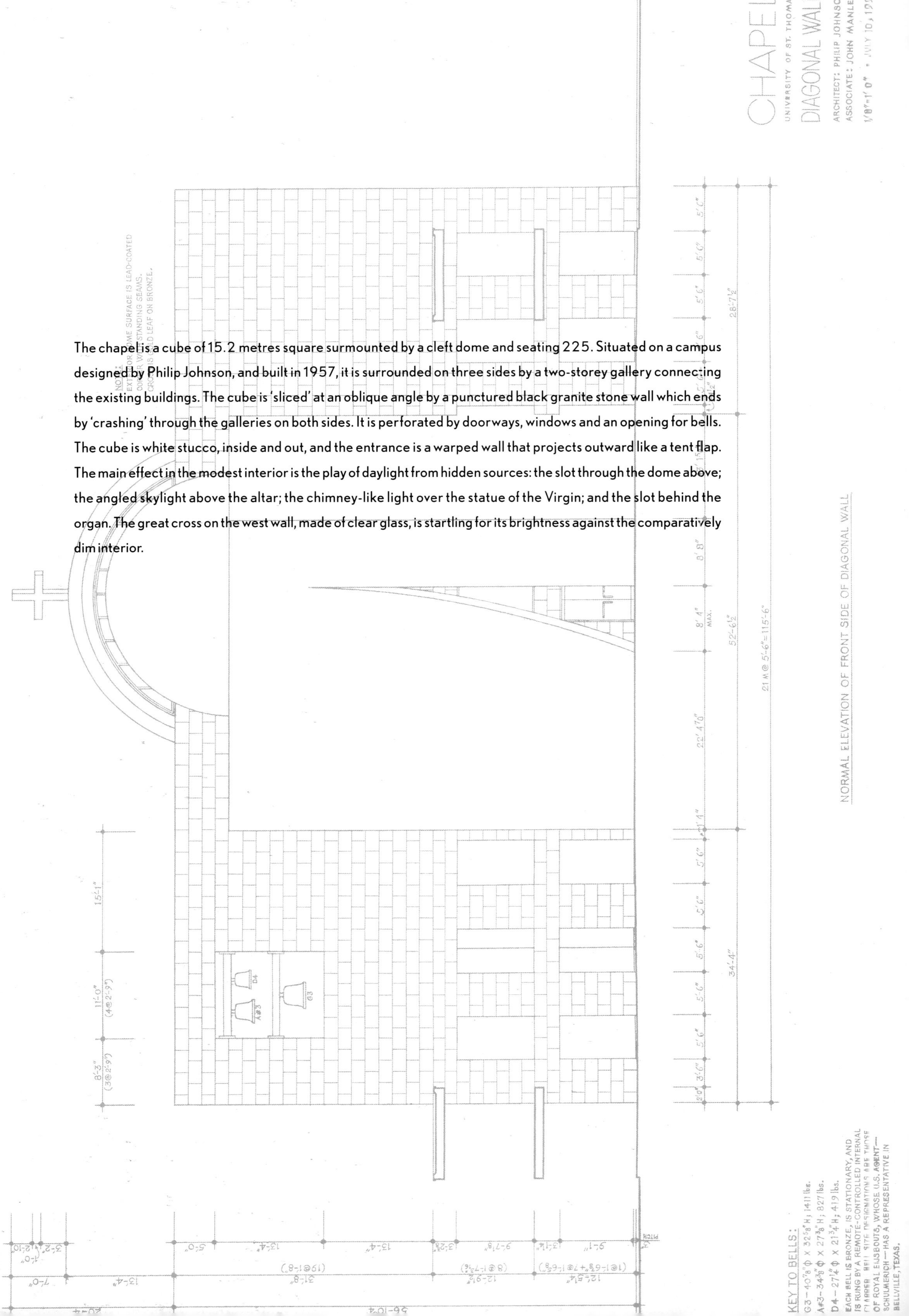

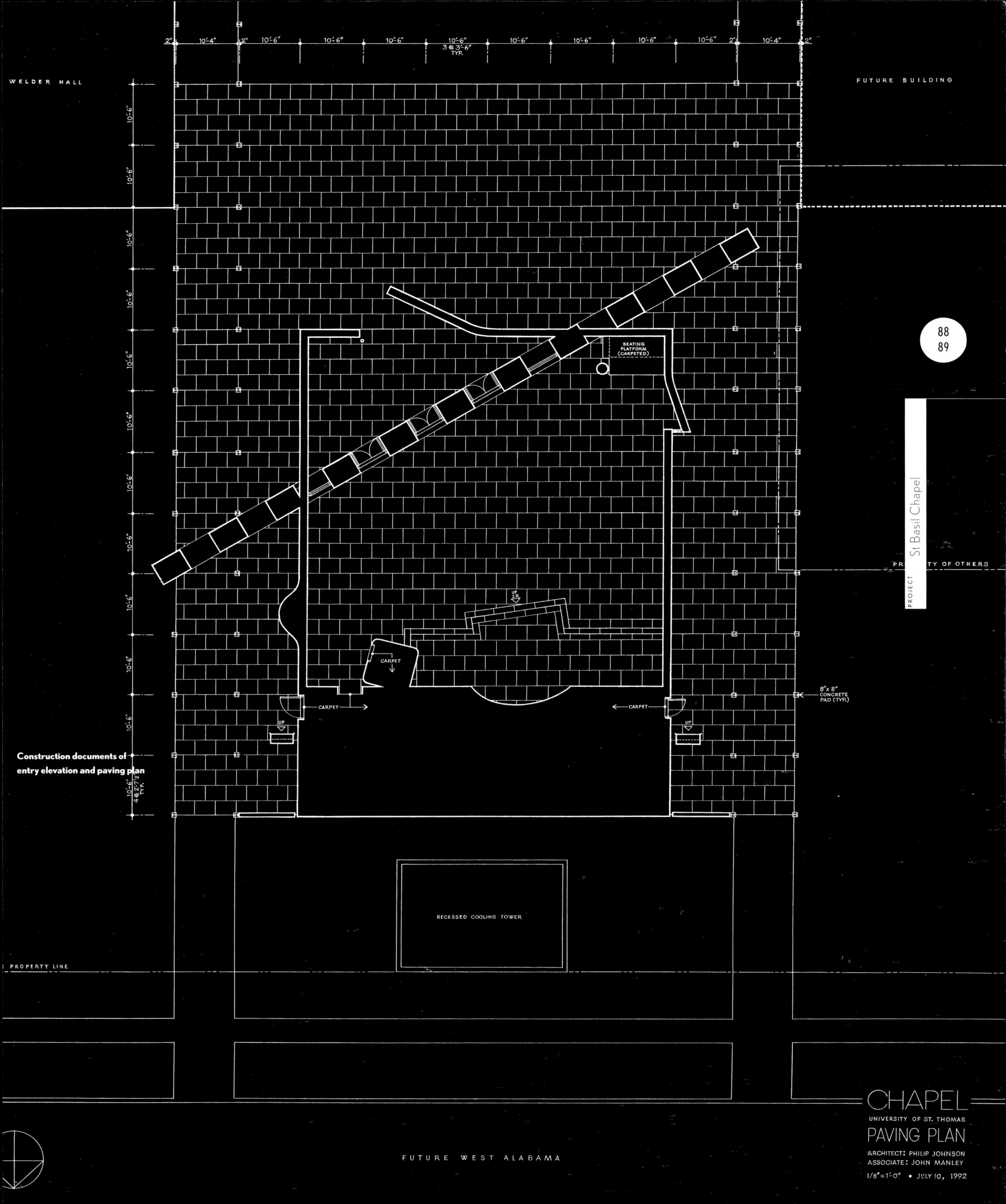

Construction documents of entry elevation and paving plan

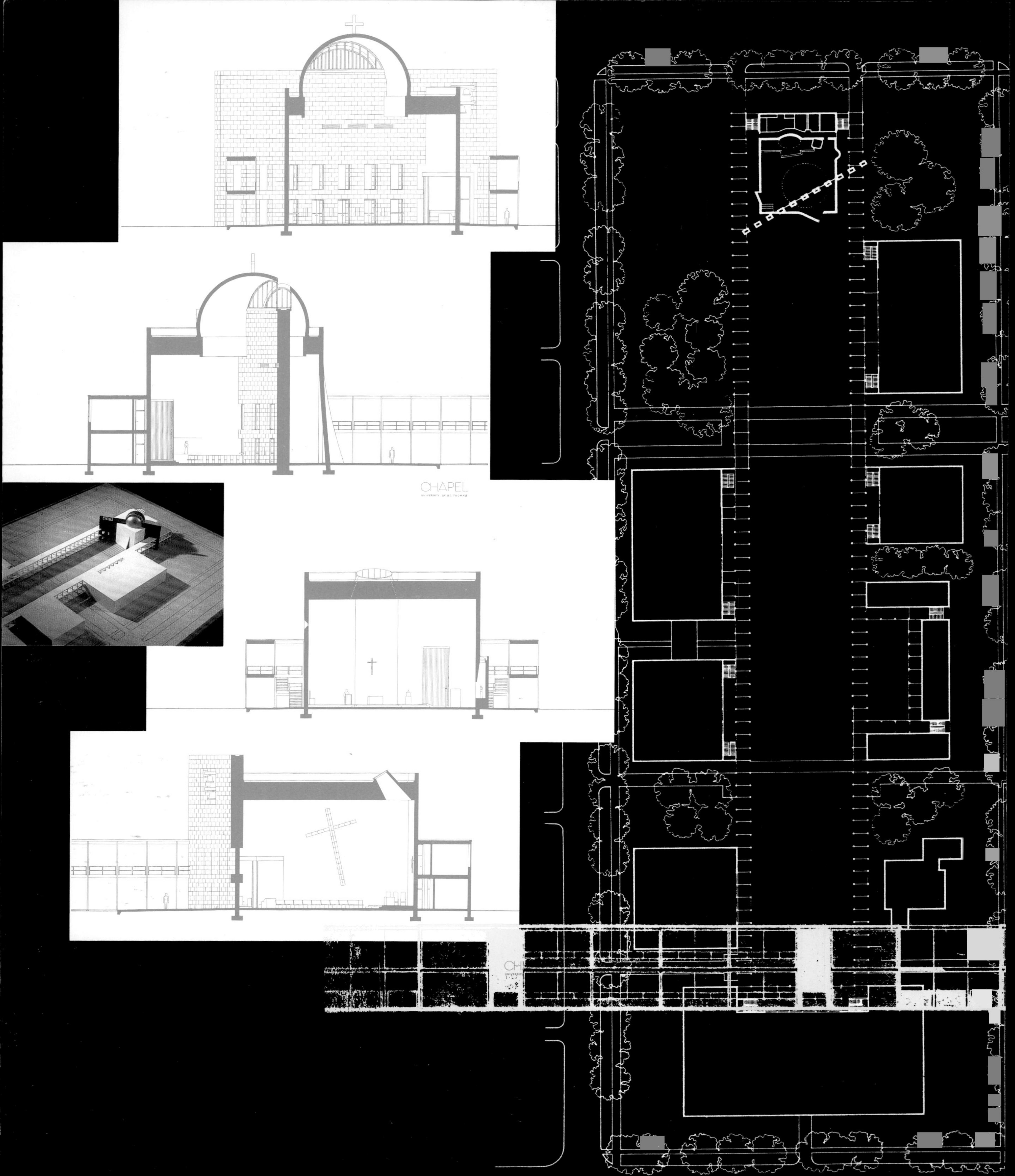
CHAPEL
UNIVERSITY OF ST. THOMAS

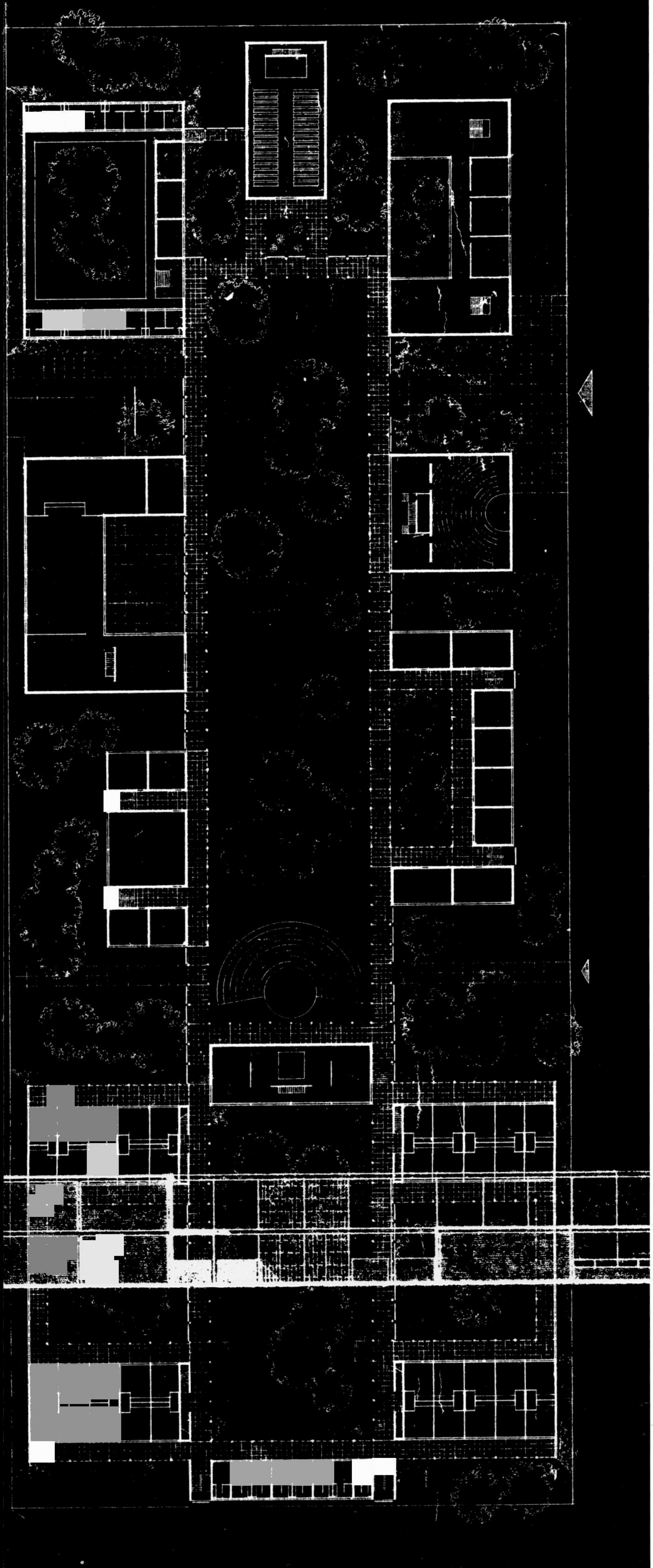

From left to right: Model of 1996; section studies of main room; final site plan; site plan of 1956 with proposed chapel; original elevation study of 1958

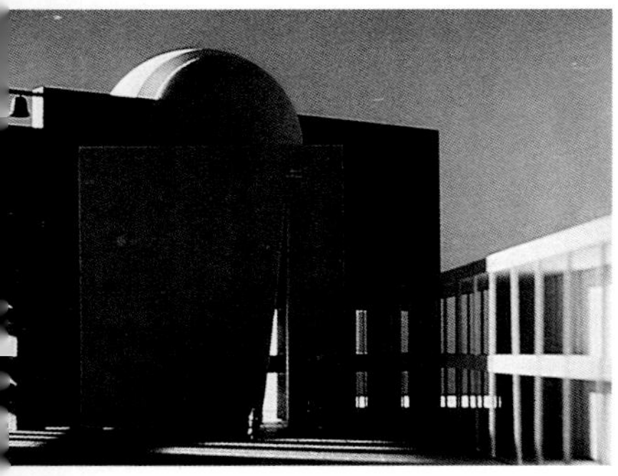

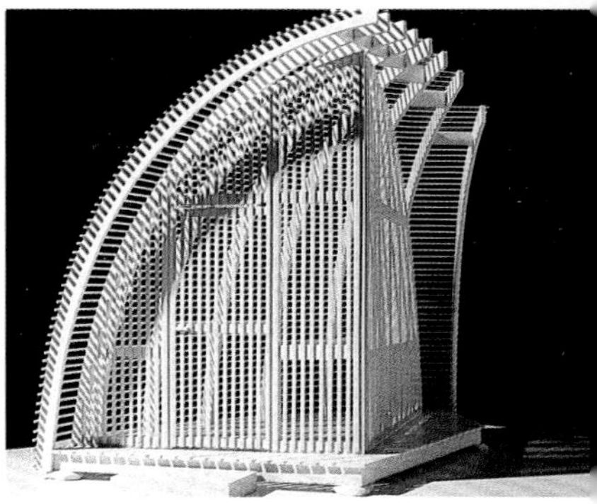

SLAT

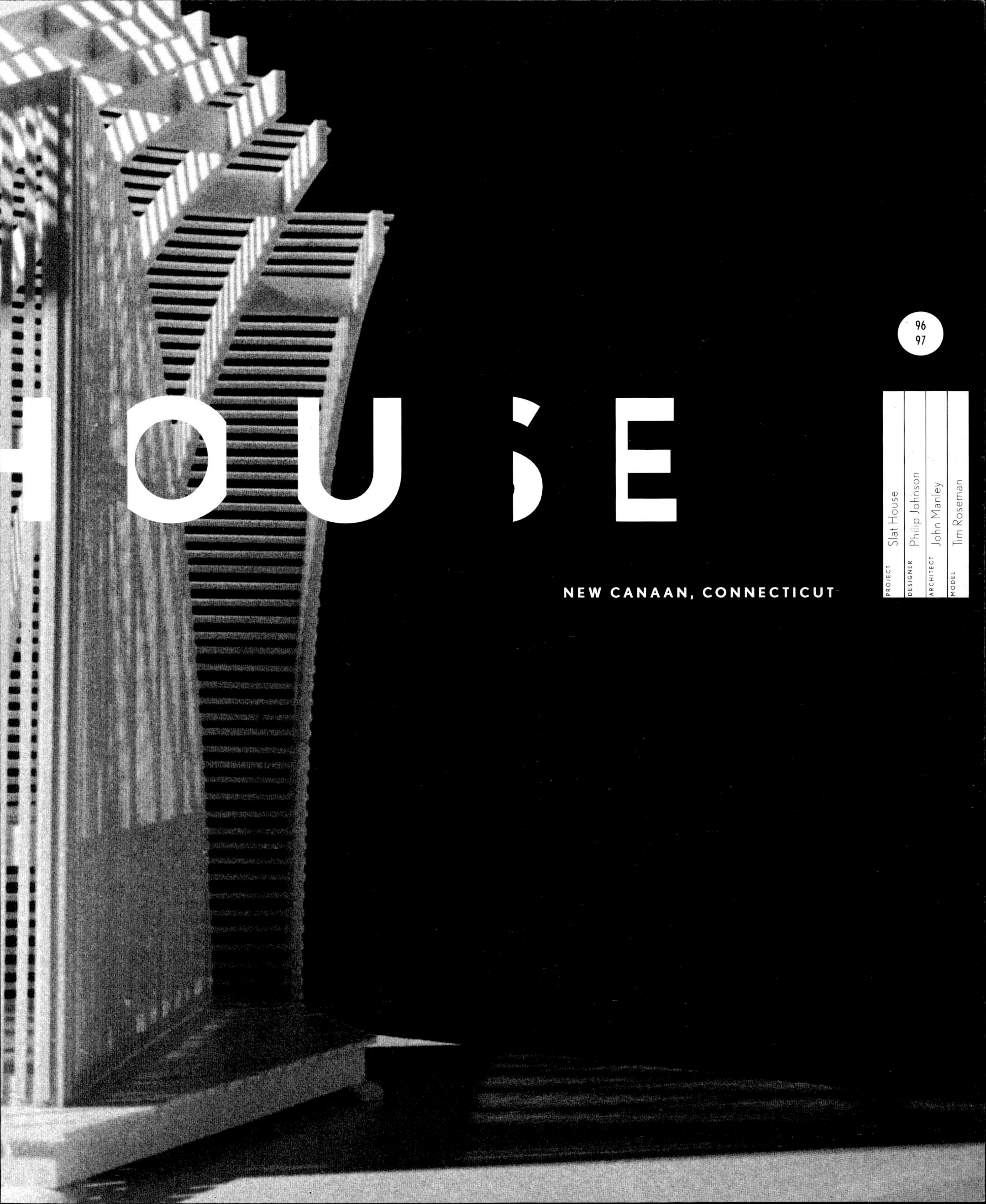

HOUSE

NEW CANAAN, CONNECTICUT

PROJECT Slat House
DESIGNER Philip Johnson
ARCHITECT John Manley
MODEL Tim Roseman

1991

The project arose from a request for a potting shed for a small residential garden. It resulted in this tiny inspirational garden folly. Approximately an eighth of a sphere and 3.65 metres in height, this small wooden enclosure faces the owner's home with its curved face and the forest with its angled side. The simple timber framing and ribs are covered with 35 x 9.5 millimetre teak slats, which create a secure enclosure with dramatic interior daylight shadow effects mirroring the visual richness of being in the centre of the nearby forest.

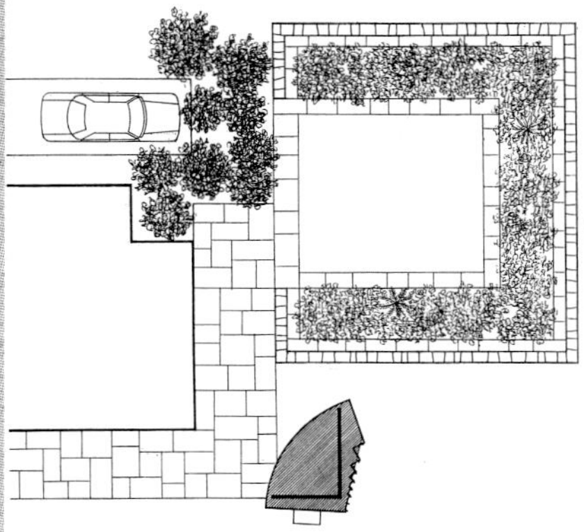

SITE PLAN

The site plan locates the Slat House between house and forest at the edge of the formal terraced garden

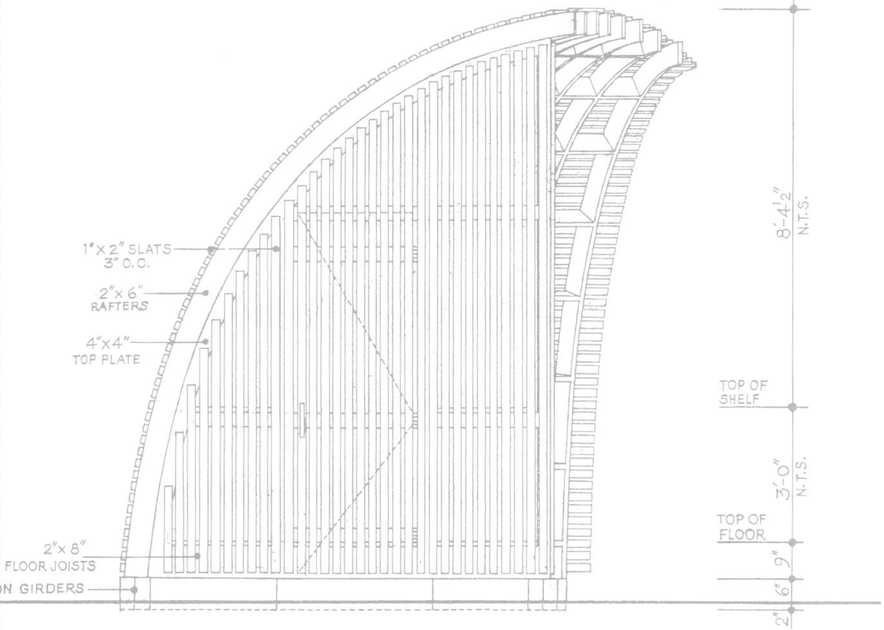

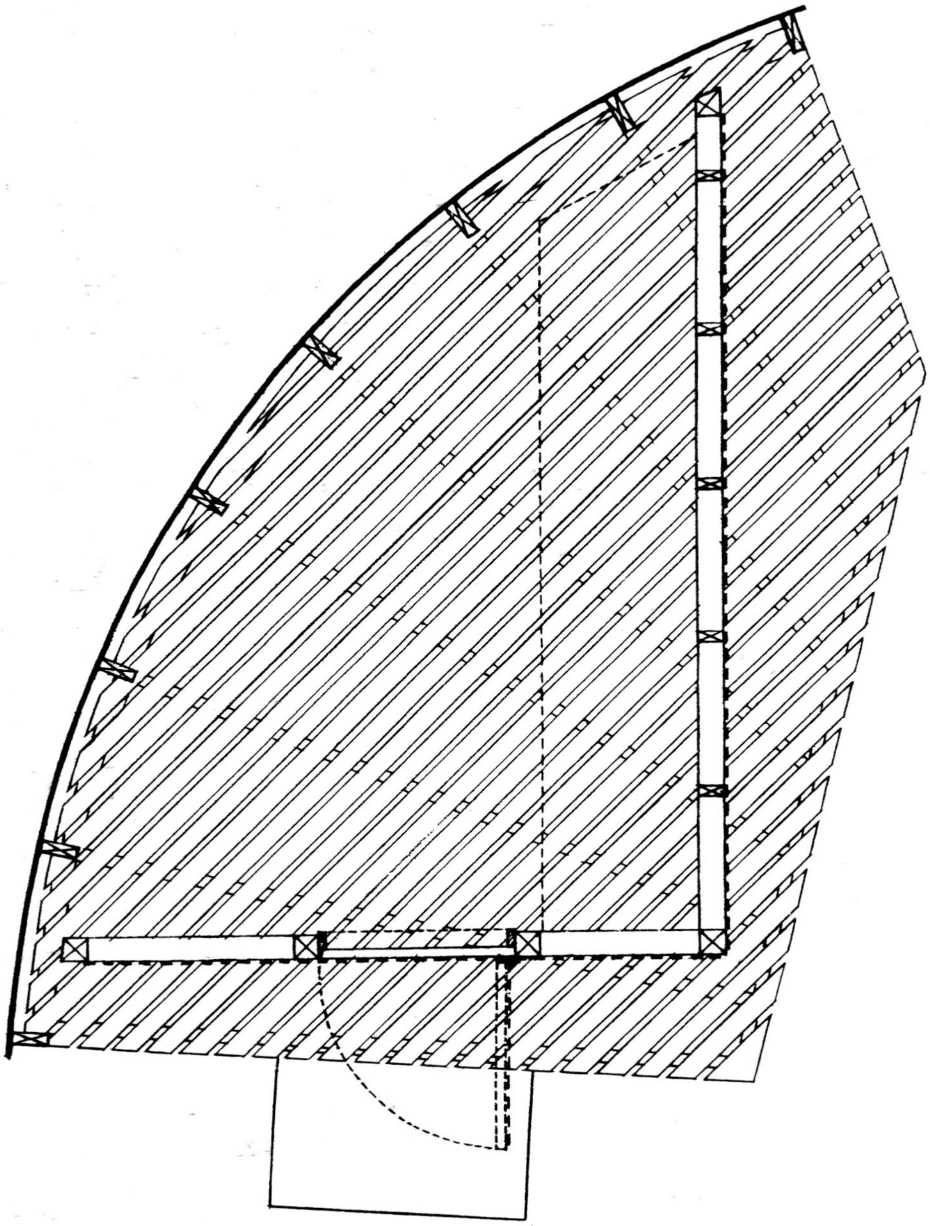

Floor Plan

PLAN/SECTION AT FLOOR LEVEL
SHOWING FLOORING

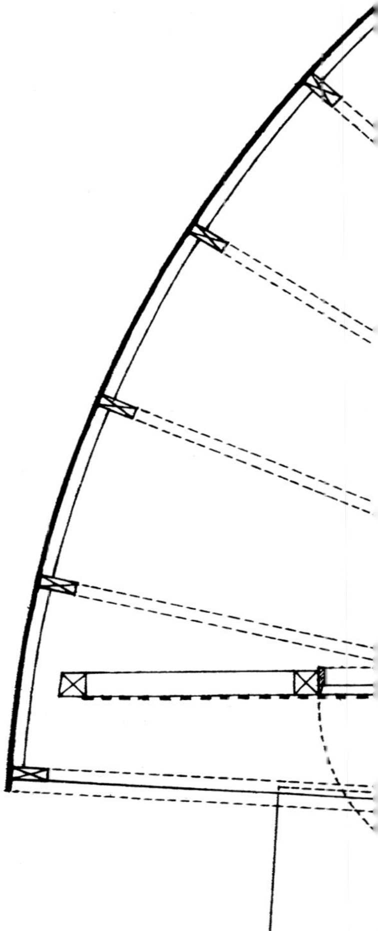

Framing Plan

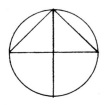

PLAN/SECT
SHOWING

September 13, 1991

LOUIS E. LEE CO.

BUILDING CONSTRUCTION

P.O. BOX 935
121 CHERRY STREET
NEW CANAAN, CONN. 06840
203 966 9553

GAZEBO

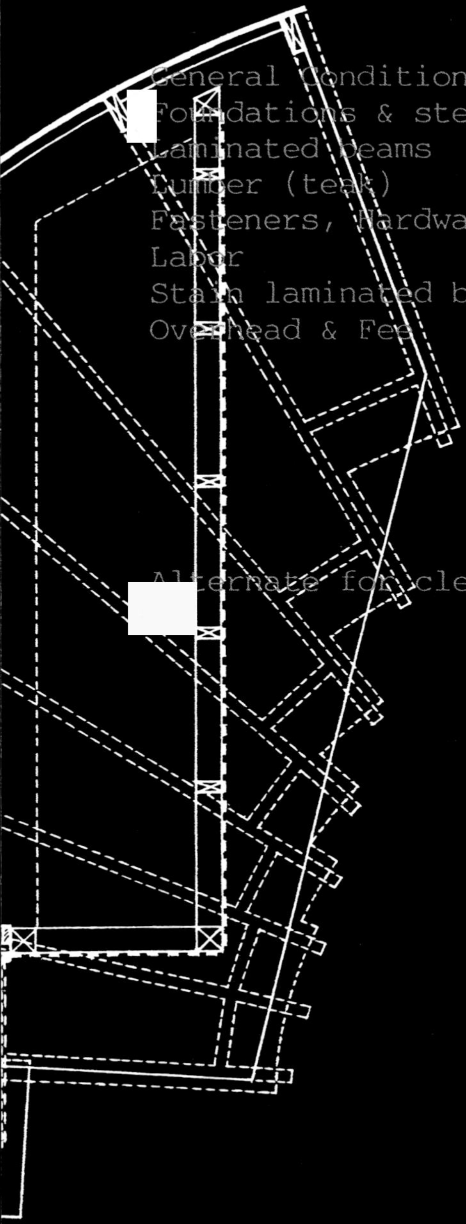

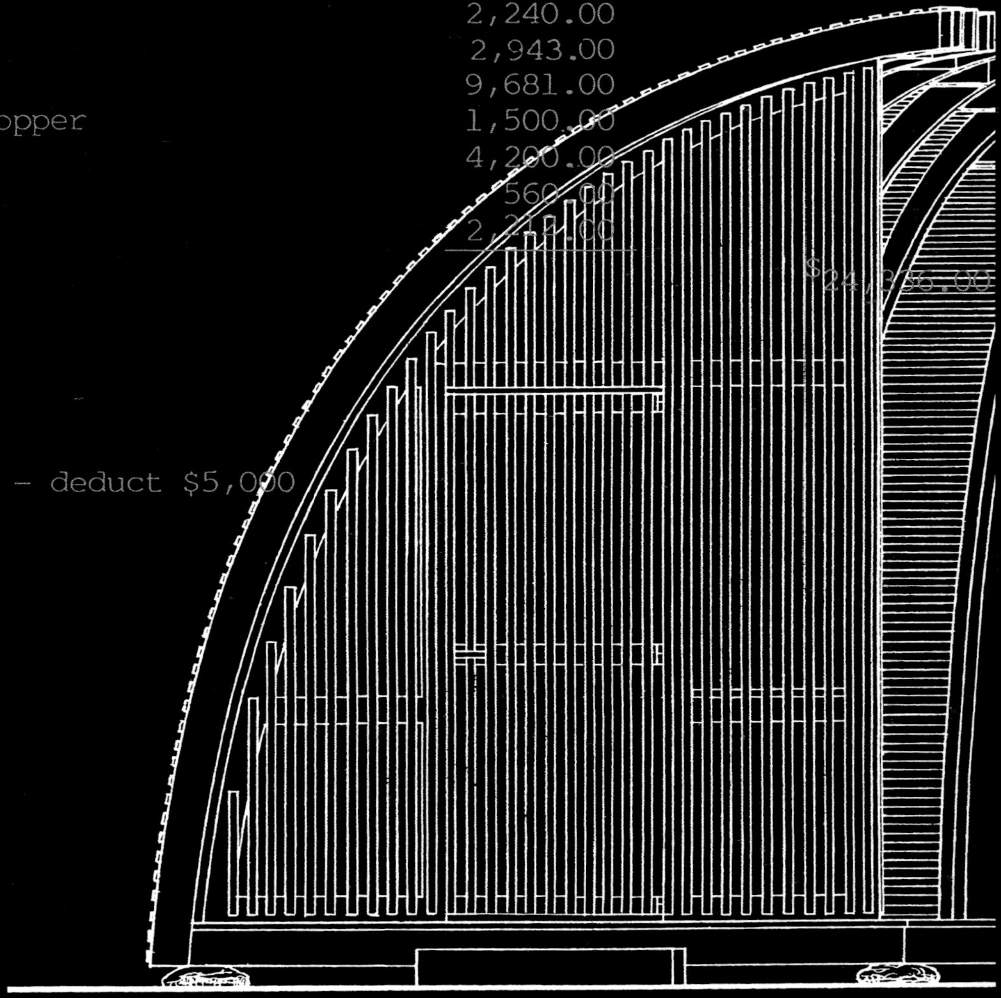

General Conditions	1,000.00
Foundations & step	2,240.00
Laminated beams	2,943.00
Lumber (teak)	9,681.00
Fasteners, Hardware & Copper	1,500.00
Labor	4,200.00
Stain laminated beams	560.00
Overhead & Fee	2,212.00
	$24,336.00

Alternate for clear fir - deduct $5,000

PROJECT Slat House

100
101

Elevation

T FLOOR LEVEL
F FRAMING

SOUTH ELEVATION

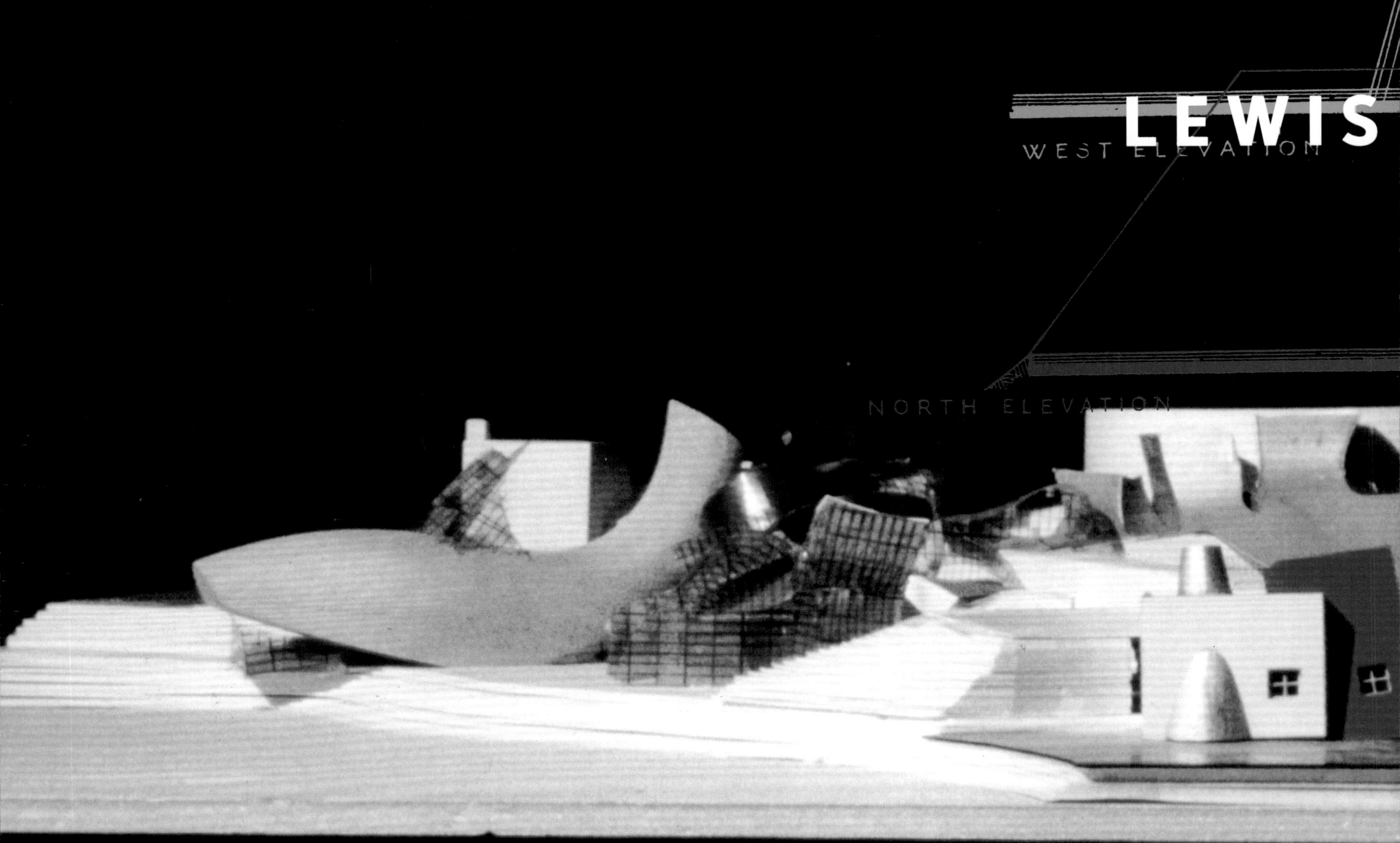
LEWIS
WEST ELEVATION
NORTH ELEVATION

GUEST HOUSE STUDIES

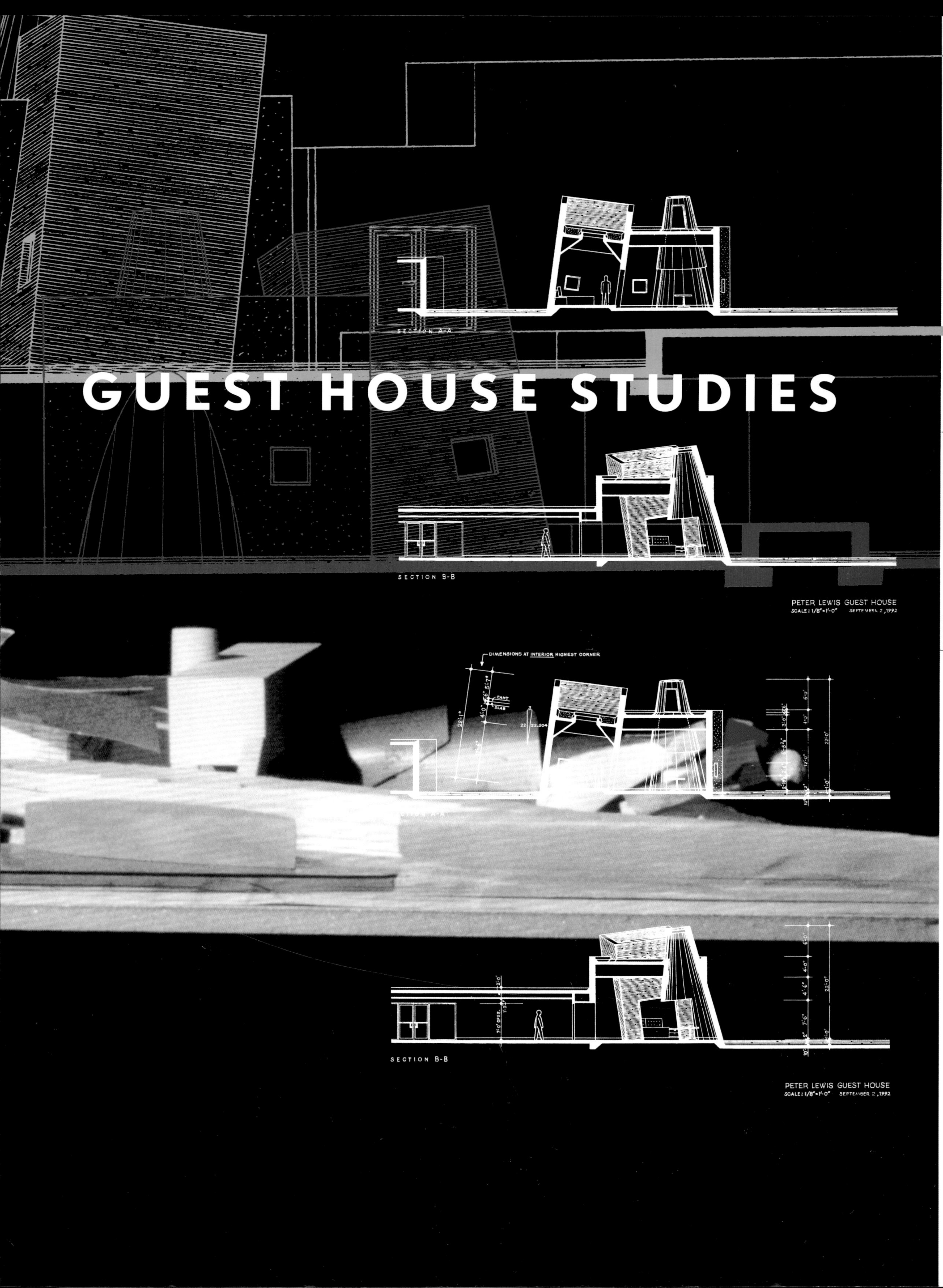

PROJECT Lewis Guest House Studies
DESIGNER Philip Johnson
ARCHITECT John Manley
MANAGER David Harrison

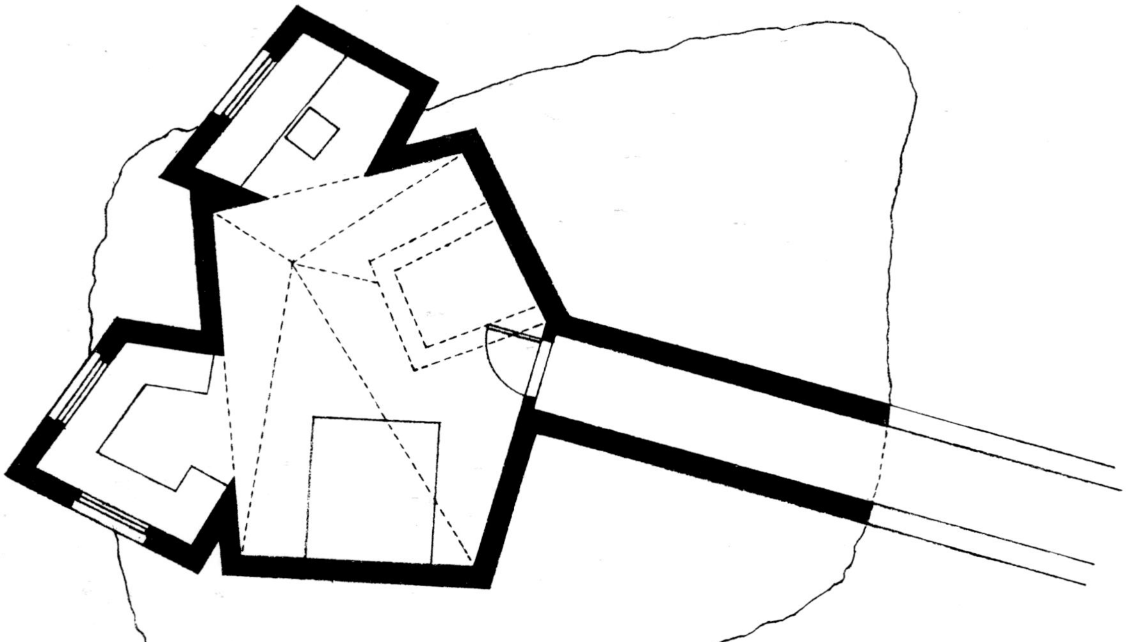

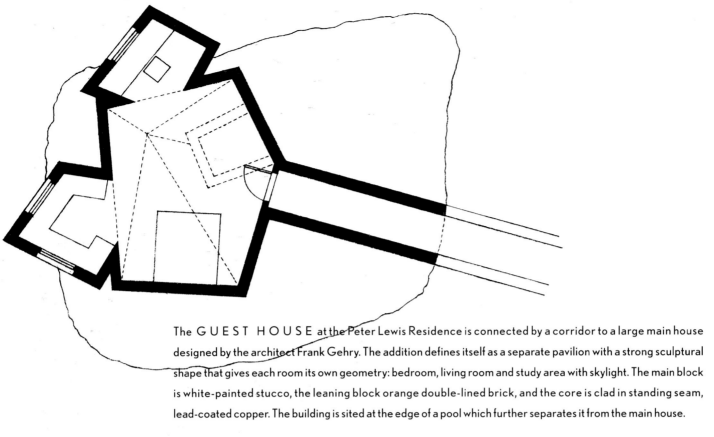

The GUEST HOUSE at the Peter Lewis Residence is connected by a corridor to a large main house designed by the architect Frank Gehry. The addition defines itself as a separate pavilion with a strong sculptural shape that gives each room its own geometry: bedroom, living room and study area with skylight. The main block is white-painted stucco, the leaning block orange double-lined brick, and the core is clad in standing seam, lead-coated copper. The building is sited at the edge of a pool which further separates it from the main house.

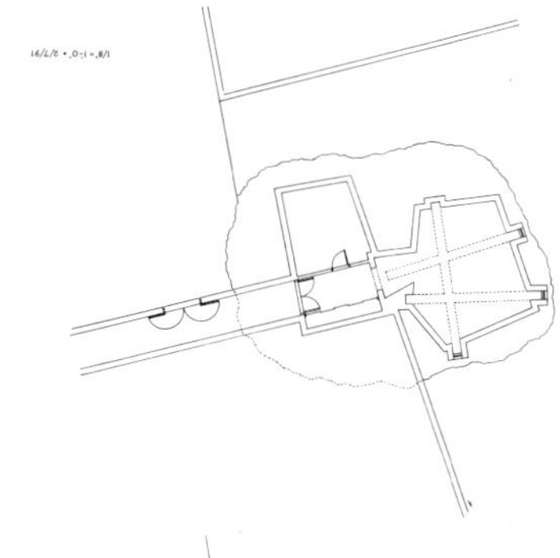

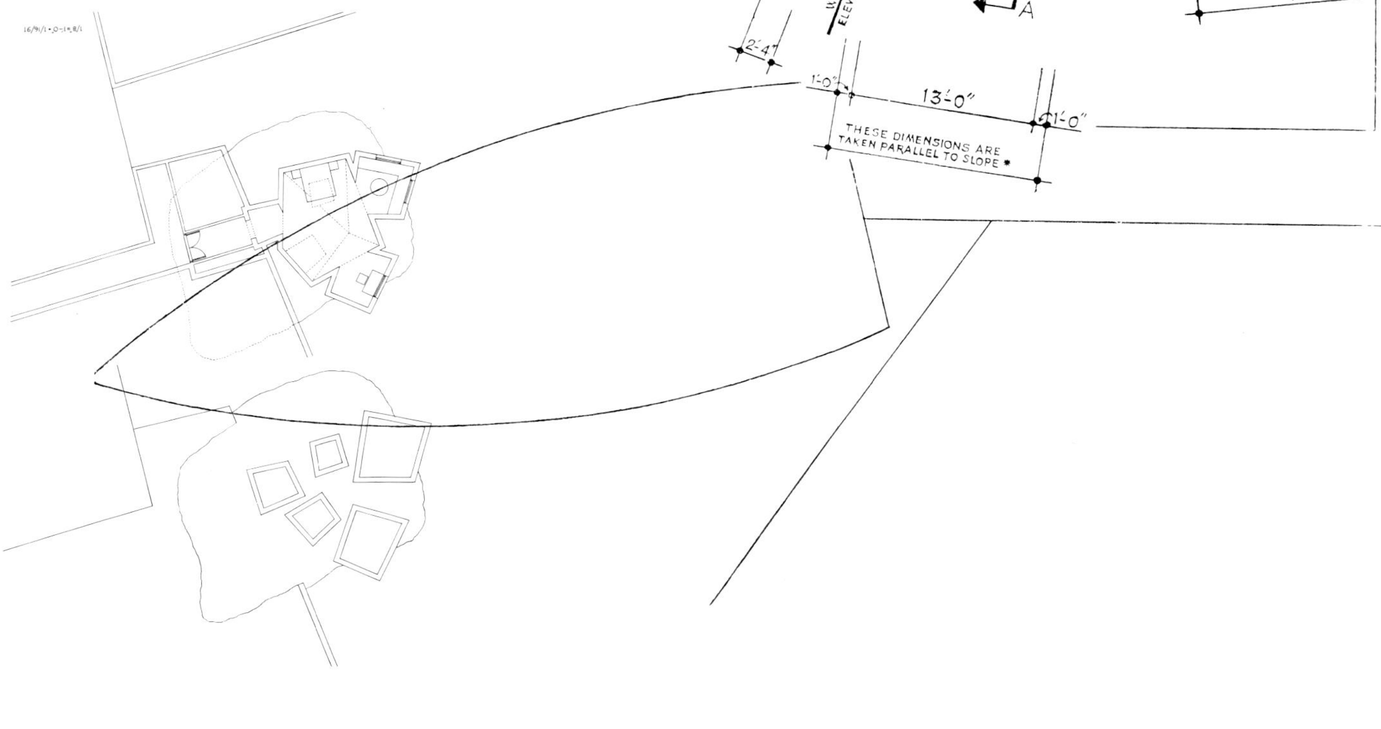

Early house in the 'Rock' studies
compared to the much later
'cone and cube' organisation

PETER LEWIS GU
SCALE: 1/8"=1'-0" • FE

The cube and the cone were
my early attempts to break down
both shapes and stuff them together.
I liked the results but
I much prefer what I got to
later in the designs for Peter Lewis's
especially #3, the Octopus all soft
and squeegy

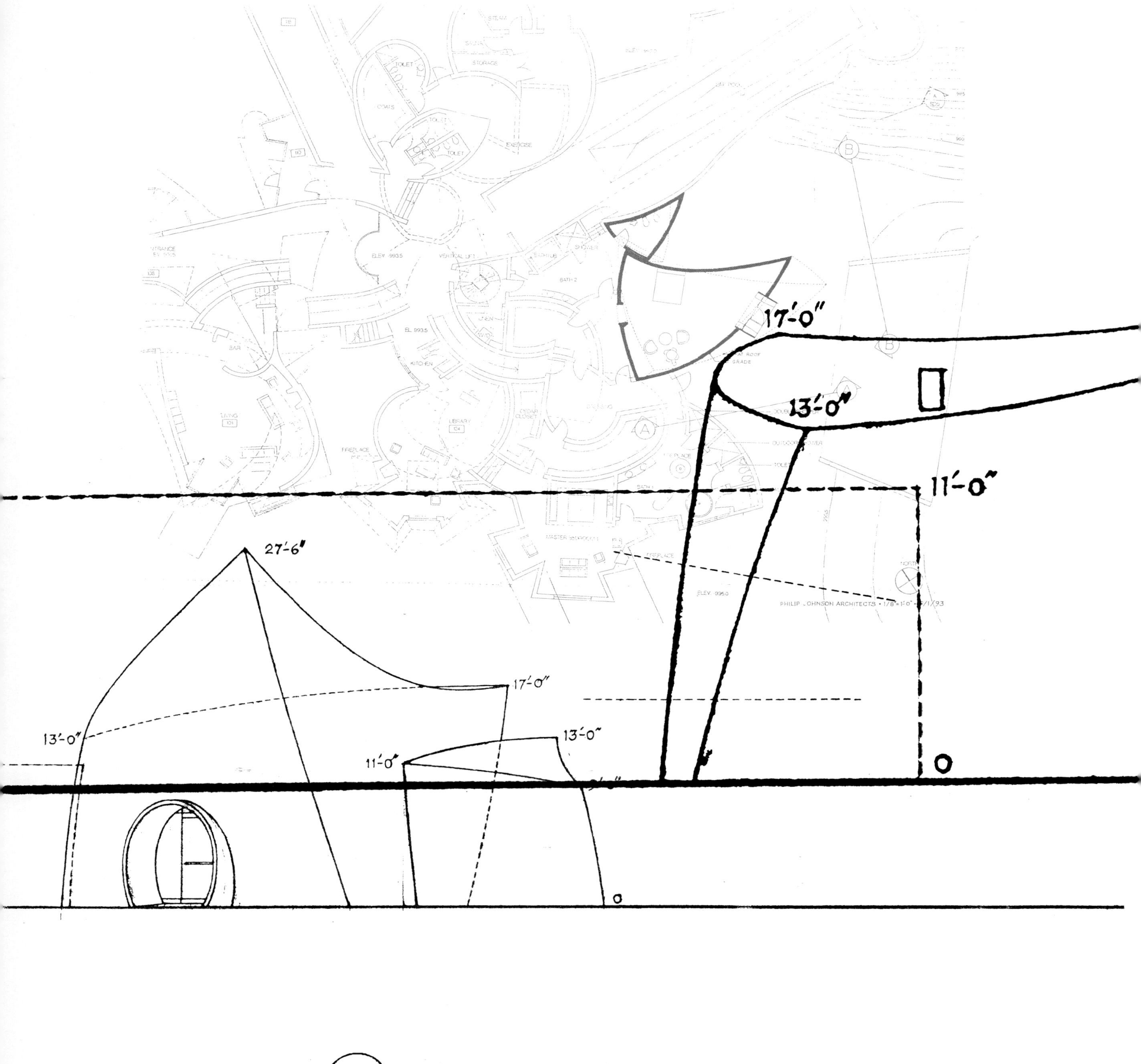

ELEVATION B

First study for addition of one room to Lewis house and sketch of 'Rock' study

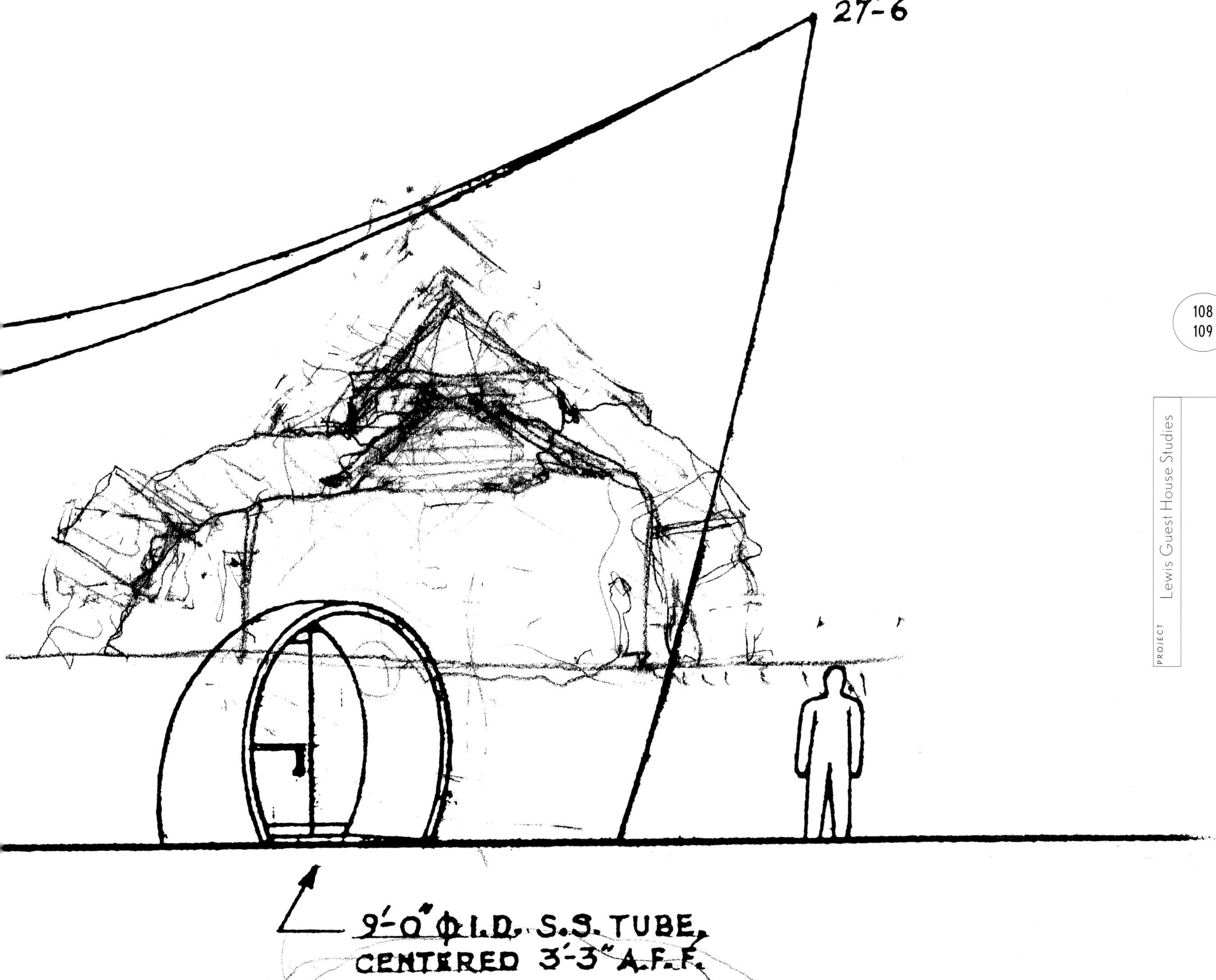
27'-6"
9'-0" Φ I.D. S.S. TUBE,
CENTERED 3'-3" A.F.F.

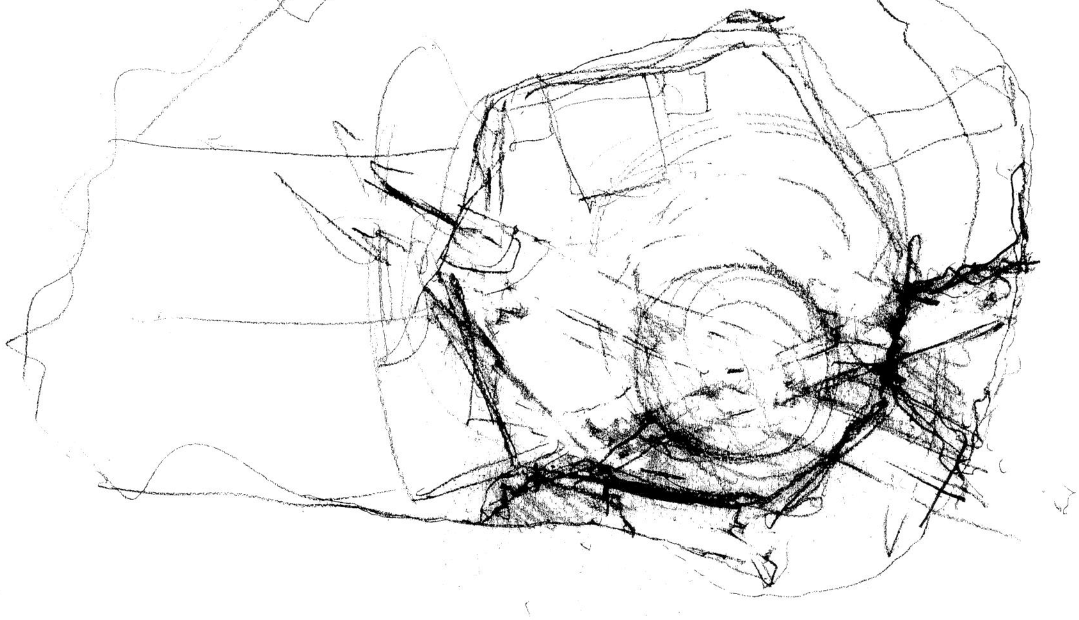

The pear in the cube was the result of my battle with Frank Gehry's computer. I lost

I took a real live pear to the machine to see how it could help me fit it into a cube. It did, the results came back within minutes Beautiful! Only the resulting room was hideously ugly.

But I really needed the computer to tell me <u>how</u> ugly

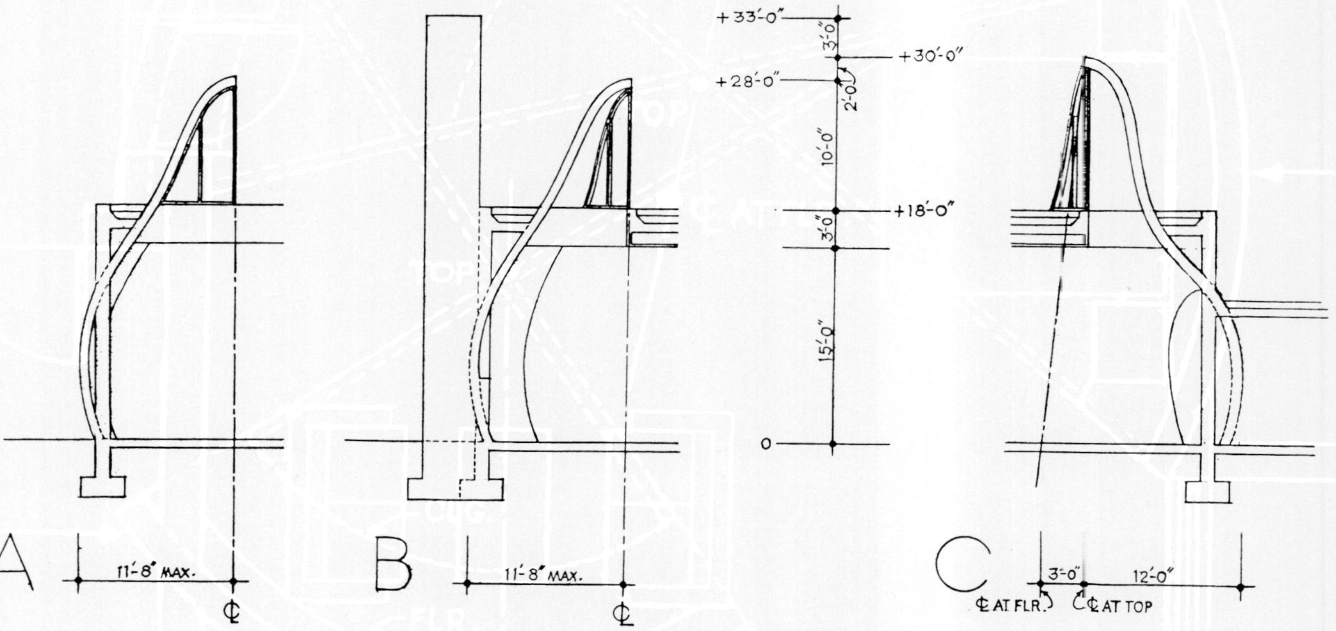

'Pear' studies: sections and plan

PUERTA DE

MADRID, SPAIN

EUROPA

PROJECT	Puerta de Europa
FIRM	John Burgee Architects
PARTNER	John Burgee
DESIGN CONSULTANT	Philip Johnson

Perspective of office towers with new low-rise housing and hotel in background

1995

PUERTA DE EUROPA is a major office and residential project which stands astride the Paseo de la Castellana, Madrid's most important boulevard, on the north side of the Plaza de Castilla. The location of the site over a subway interchange makes it structurally impossible for the office buildings to stand near the street. In order for the two towers to read as a pair, and to ensure their visibility from up and down the Paseo, they have been designed to lean toward each other over their plazas. This bold move creates a portal which, being at the northern end of the business district, becomes the gateway to Europe, hence the name of the project. The facade of each tower is a composition of a major structural grid of rectilinear and diagonal members clad in stainless steel, and minor grid painted red. These elements stand out from a simple grey glass curtain wall.

Site plan and model

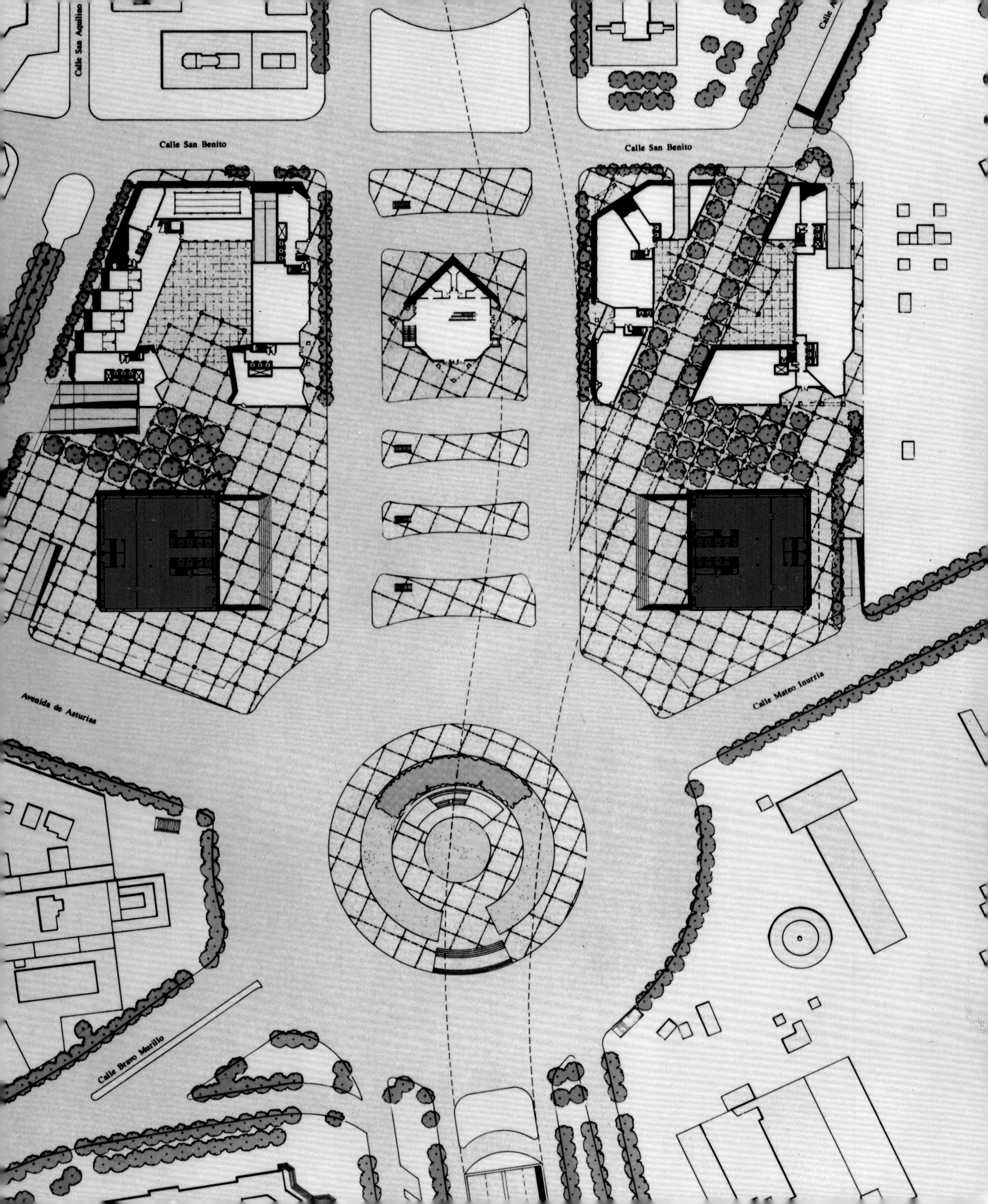

Calle San Aquilino
Calle San Benito
Calle San Benito
Calle
Avenida de Asturias
Calle Mateo Inurria
Calle Bravo Murillo

These buildings are a strange amalgam of Baroque gateway to the city and a Constructivist exercise. The aim was to express Baroque Madrid to call attention to the great axis of the city.

But the actual design came from Alexander Rodchenko the great Soviet constructivist specifically from the now lost painting. Isn't it LINE.

Alexander Rodchenko, book cover for 'Zaumniki', by Kruchenykh, Petnikov and Khlebnikov, 1922

Sequence of construction

Puerta de Europa

Summary of structure The two leaning towers of Puerta de Europa form a portal or gate framing the Paseo de la Castellana, the great north-south artery of Madrid. The buildings have plan dimensions of 35.105 metres (in the direction of the cantilever) by 36.090 metres (transverse to the cantilever). Each office floor is displaced 1013 millimetres from the floor below. The building slope and plan dimensions were developed so as to properly organise the curtain wall. Each building has twenty-four office floors and one plant room floor above the plaza. Additionally, a roof-top heliport is located on the parapet level.

Other statistics Building slope 14.3 degrees +;
Height above the plaza 113.56 metres;
Height above the basement 123.76 metres;
Floor-to-floor height 3.97 metres

Special requirements While all building systems must incorporate an adequate level of lateral stiffness and strength, a leaning building must have significantly increased stiffness in the direction of the cantilever. That is, in addition to the need to resist the normal lateral forces from wind and earthquake, the system must resist also the gravity-induced overturning moment, and must do so at very low levels of lateral deflection. This enhanced requirement is particularly severe in that the gravity-induced lateral deflection may not be recoverable: such deflection may remain permanently in the structure and, in concrete structures, may increase with time on account of the long-term (creep) properties of concrete.

Post-tensions Clearly, post-tensioning is a proven technique for the control of gravity-induced deflection, although it has not been used in the specific application required for the towers of Puerta de Europa. Conceptually, post-tensioning is introduced into those elements of the structural system that are under gravity-induced tension so as to place these members in compression. By locating the post-tensioning system in the outer (tension) wall of the building, it is possible to compensate for all or a part of the lateral deflection induced by gravity loading.

Post-tensioning creates an increased efficiency of the structural system by allowing a reduction in required stiffness, thus reducing cost.

Structural description The structural systems for the twin towers of Puerta de Europa were selected in response to consideration of exterior aesthetic, anticipated architectural layout of interior spaces, cost, time of construction and by other considerations outside of the control of the structural engineer.

Systems description Floor slabs in office areas are 85-millimetre-thick lightweight concrete over 60-millimetre-deep profiled metal deck. Floor slabs at Planta Baja and below are of stone concrete, with conventional forming. Beams and girders are of structural steel with yield points ranging from 250 MPa to 350 MPa. With a floor-to-floor height of 3970 millimetres, a ceiling height of 3000 millimetres, and electrified raised floor of 130 millimetres and the 145 millimetres slab/deck assembly, the depths of beams are heavily constrained. Accordingly, nearly all beams and girders are located on the architectural module so as to allow light fixtures to nestle between the floor framing. Even so, most of the floor beams are notched to allow passage of ductwork and the flange width of girders is restricted. Columns are of structural steel (250 MPa to 450 MPa); some columns in below grade areas are encased in concrete.

The service core is of reinforced concrete. The structural design allowed for slip forming, sliding forms, jumped forms and the like. The contractor chose the slip form technique.

A tie-down ballast of reinforced concrete is used to provide an adequate factor of safety against overturning. The ballast is 50 metres long, 12.4 metres wide and 9.6 metres deep, weighing 14,000 tons.

Post-tensioning, while used here for composite concrete and structural steel, is a conventional system, manufactured for use in post-tensioned concrete construction. For physical protection, the post-tensioning is carried in steel pipes, not post-tensioning ducts. The system is anchored in the concrete ballast and again at the top of the parapet.

The basic deflection control operation takes place at the parapet level.

The foundations are cast in-situ barrettes (elongated piles).

A diaphragm wall forms the perimeter of the excavation and is part of, and is used to form, the tie-down ballast.

The lateral force resisting system consists of braced frames in structural steel placed in each of the four exterior walls.

To mobilise the stiffening influence of the intrinsic triangulation of the facade, roof-top stiffening trusses, 7.9 metres deep, frame the depth of the plan room space.

Two interior frames are provided, both using the concrete services core. These frames have three more or less independent components: the triangulation consisting of a vertical (a steel column) and the structural steel diagonal; the triangulation consisting of a vertical (the concrete services core) and the structural steel diagonal; the cantilever stiffness of the services core.

The exterior and the interior frames are forced to have virtually the same lateral deflection by the stiffening influence of the concrete floors acting as horizontal diaphragms. To the extent that differences exist in the stiffness characteristics of the frames (ie, the deformed shape of the frame), large shear stresses are introduced into those diaphragms.

Leslie E Robertson
Leslie E Robertson Associates, Engineers

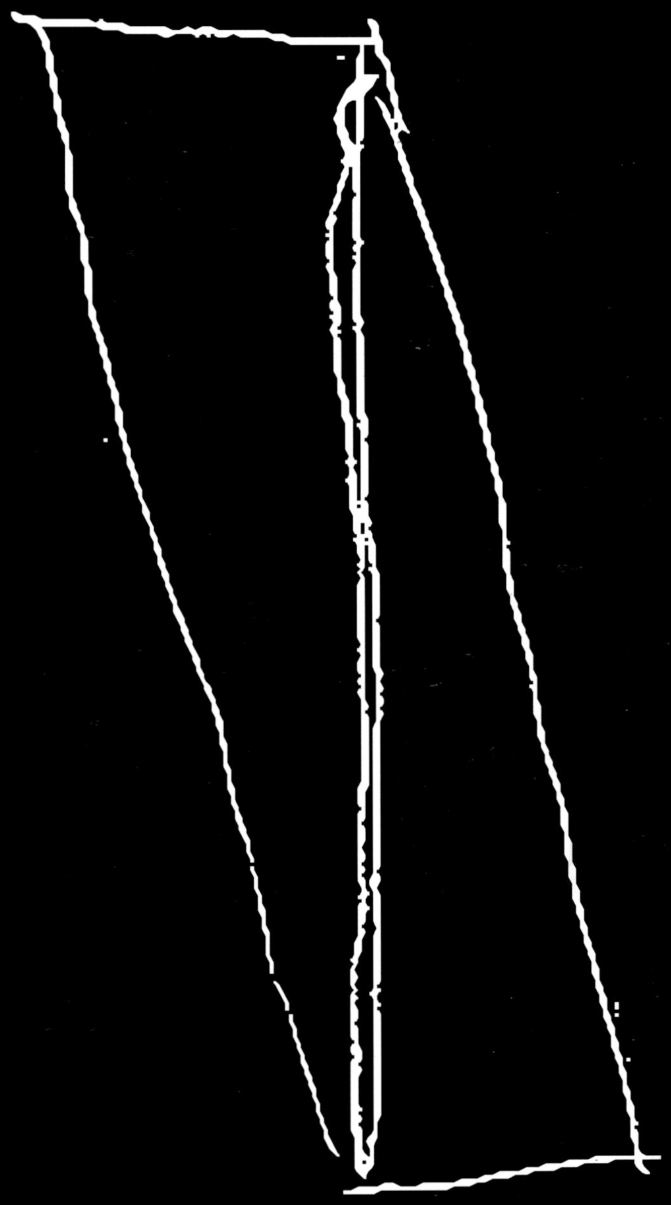

PARTNER, PHILIP JOHNSON, RITCHIE & FIORE ARCHITECTS

PHILIP JOHNSON FAIA

Philip Johnson has played a decisive role in American architecture in the twentieth century. Through his designs, writings and teaching, he has helped to define the changing theoretical discourse and built form taken by architecture during the last sixty-five years.

As founder and director of the Museum of Modern Art's Department of Architecture, Philip Johnson and architectural historian Henry-Russell Hitchcock mounted the landmark 1932 exhibition entitled 'The International Style'.

In advocating the practice and benefits of the International Style, Philip Johnson created two of its most important monuments, the Seagram Building (1958) with Mies van der Rohe and his own Glass House (1949) in Connecticut.

Philip Johnson has had a long productive career as an architect. With his partner John Burgee he designed the AT&T Corporate Headquarters in New York (1984). With its stone cladding and use of traditional ornament, it became a controversial exemplar of Post-Modern design. For over twenty years Johnson & Burgee produced dramatic buildings in every major city in the United States.

In 1988, Philip Johnson organised an exhibition with Mark Wigley at the Museum of Modern Art entitled 'Deconstructivist Architecture'. It presented the work of seven young architects who were exploring forms and organisations that directly confronted and contradicted the idealism of the Modern Movement and the historicism of Post-Modern thought.

In continuing to explore this phenomenon of a non-Euclidean order and 'wanton' forms, Philip Johnson, in his new partnership with Alan Ritchie and David Fiore, has designed the 'last' building on his Connecticut estate. The Gate House (1995) with its warped planes and distorted geometry represents the latest theme in his long career; a career in which the only constant is a passionate belief in the art of architecture and the inevitability of change.

LIST OF PROJECTS

TURNING POINT

Philip Johnson, Ritchie & Fiore Architects
Project Designer Philip Johnson
Partner in Charge David Fiore
Project Architect Elizabeth Murrell
Completion Date 1996
Photographer Robert Walker
Model Elizabeth Murrell

GATE HOUSE

Philip Johnson Architects
Project Designer Philip Johnson
Project Architect John Manley
Project Manager David Harrison
Computer Drafting Yasin Abdullah
Completion Date 1995
Photographers Michael Moran, Robert Walker, David Harrison
Model Joe Santeramo
Structural Engineer Ysrael A Seinuk, PC

BERLIN ALTERNATIVE

Philip Johnson Architects
Project Designer Philip Johnson
Project Architect John Manley
Associate Architects Pysall, Stahrenberg & Partners
Computer Drafting Richard Schneider
Project Date 1993
Photographer Robert Walker
Model Joe Santeramo

LEWIS GUEST HOUSE

Philip Johnson, Ritchie & Fiore Architects
Project Designer Philip Johnson
Partner in Charge David Fiore
Project Architect John Manley
Project Manager David Harrison
Computer Drafting Yasin Abdullah, Ling Li
Main House Architect Frank O Gehry & Associates
Project Date 1995
Photographer Robert Walker
Model Frank O Gehry & Associates, Joe Santeramo
Structural Engineer Ysrael A Seinuk, PC

NATIONAL MUSEUM OF KOREA

Philip Johnson, Ritchie & Fiore Architects
Project Designer Philip Johnson
Partner in Charge Alan Ritchie
Project Manager Christian Bjone
Project Architect Elizabeth Murrell
Computer Drafting Ling Li

Associate Architects Anderson & Oh, Inc, Chicago, Illinois
Principal in Charge Sae Oh
Managing Principal Neil Anderson

Korean Associates Wong-Il Ltd Architects & Engineers
Partner in Charge Chung E Lee
Project Date 1995
Photographer Michael Rogul
Model Tenguerian Models, Inc
Renderer Yong H Ki
Structural Engineers Tylk, Gustafson & Associates, Inc

SETON HILL FINE ARTS CENTER

Philip Johnson Architects
Project Designer Philip Johnson
Project Architect John Manley
Project Managers Don Porter, David Harrison
Architect Duane Schrempp
Project Date 1990
Photographer Wolfgang Hoyt
Model Joe Santeramo
Structural Engineers Leslie E Robertson Associates Engineers

LAW CENTER ADDITION

Philip Johnson Architects
Project Designer Philip Johnson
Senior Designer John Manley
Project Manager Don Porter
Project Date 1991
Photographer Richard Payne
Model Joe Santeramo
Renderer Brett Bothwell

ST BASIL CHAPEL

Philip Johnson, Ritchie & Fiore Architects
Project Designer Philip Johnson
Partner in Charge David Fiore
Project Architect John Manley
Associate Architects Merriman Holt Architects
Completion Date 1996
Photographer Richard Payne
Model Joe Santeramo
Structural Engineers Cagley, Conti & Jumper

SLAT HOUSE

Philip Johnson Architects
Project Designer Philip Johnson
Project Architect John Manley
Project Date 1991
Photographer Robert Walker
Model Tim Roseman

LEWIS GUEST HOUSE STUDIES

Philip Johnson Architects
Project Designer Philip Johnson
Project Architect John Manley
Main House Architects Frank O Gehry & Associates
Project Date 1993
Models Frank O Gehry & Associates, Joe Santeramo

PUERTA DE EUROPA

John Burgee Architects
Partner in Charge John Burgee
Project Architect K Jeffrey Sydness
Design Consultant Philip Johnson
Project Manager Kurt Offer
Architect Duane Schrempp
Completion Date 1995
Structural Engineers Leslie E Robertson Associates Engineers
Director of Design Leslie E Robertson
Project Director Rick Zottola
Project Manager Monica Svojski
Renderer Howard Associates
Photographers Hedrich Blessing, Robert Royal, Isabel Colbrand